Old-Fashioned

Values

Matter

Jack Bush
And Frank Ball

Old-Fashioned Values Matter
By Jack Bush
And Frank Ball

First Printing

Published by:
Roaring Lambs Publishing
17110 Dallas Parkway, Suite 260
Dallas, TX 75248
Email: **info@RoaringLambs.org**

Dedication

My son, do not forget my teaching,
but keep my commands in your heart,
for they will prolong your life many years
and bring you peace and prosperity.
— Proverbs 3:1–2

For my grandchildren,
and everyone who wants to keep
past strengths that will
help them live better today
and build a better future.

Values

For where your treasure is,
there your heart will be also.
— Luke 12:34

What we value governs our behavior
and determines whether we will have
a positive or negative impact
in the world where we live.

Acknowledgements

For the many folks who brought inspiration and help, thank you.

Roaring Lambs

Years ago, I started attending the Roaring Lambs recognition dinners. They were very special occasions. Then we joined their chapter-by-chapter Bible study group that has met every Sunday morning for about forty years.

Roaring Lambs believe that values really do matter. They think people should give serious thought to what they value, and I agree.

Values are an important aspect of faith. The Bible is filled with value principles. God sees our hearts and is always measuring our progress, treasuring what matters most—to "bear much fruit" (John 15:8).

The Roaring Lambs mission seeks to amplify our faith—to raise our enthusiasm from silent testimonies to much higher levels—so we can ROAR.

Changing Values

Graduating high school seniors cannot imagine life without computers and cell phones. They will enter adult society with a modern definition of love, honesty, and integrity. What little they know of the past seems obsolete and therefore irrelevant. The values I treasure are often unimportant to them, and that makes me want to roar.

If I don't speak up, my grandkids will never know what I have learned from decades past. I thank the Roaring Lambs for giving me the motivation to sit down and write about some of my values.

Overrated Statistics

We now live in an information age when just about any argument can be supported with statistics from somewhere. The truth is often obscured by the media pleasing its audience by reporting claims without fact checking.

Obviously, information in this book came from somewhere. I accumulated piles of papers, clippings, and books in an effort to add substance to my perceptions. My decades of experience have been valuable to many, because I weigh my opinions carefully against many supporter and detractors.

You may do what I know you will do anyway: embrace my words when you find them helpful and ignore the rest.

Thank you for allowing me this opportunity to ROAR.

Good Stuff

Garry Kinder was the Roaring Lambs Bible Study teacher for over thirty-eight years. "Good stuff," he would roar when he expressed his opinion of a biblical value he really liked.

I sincerely pray that you will find some "good stuff" in this book.

Foreword

As the heavens are higher than the earth, so are my ways
higher than your ways and my thoughts than your thoughts.
— Isaiah 55:9

Human Values

Everybody has them—people, governments, businesses,
ministries—every organization and individual. Some values are
better than others. Some are constructive. Others are destructive.

God's Values

The Bible is more than just the Ten Commandments. Story after
story reveals God's character and the principles we're given to live
by, not to imprison us but to free us to enjoy the fullness of life.
Jesus taught through parables and precepts that would work well
for us today, if we would take those lessons to heart.

Changing Values

After the Supreme Court made its landmark judgment in 1962, our
nation removed prayer from the classrooms. No longer could the
Ten Commandments be on public display lest someone read and
follow them instead of doing what was "right in their own eyes"
(which the Bible condemned in Numbers 15:39).

In the decades that followed, our society has gradually distanced
itself from the Ten Commandments and the godly principles that
have defined righteousness for thousands of years.

During my lifetime, some values have changed drastically, and I
fear that the peace and joy we have known since the birth of Christ
will continue to fade. If enough of us will stand up for the Christian

values that our nation was founded upon, we might reverse that trend.

Preaching is good for those who will listen, but I believe we best dispel the darkness by letting our lights shine. That is why I wanted to write this book—to reveal some treasured lessons of my history and let my light shine.

Old-Fashioned Values

If you've spent time with your grandfather, you've probably had times when you thought he was "old-fashioned" in his beliefs and values. I can understand that, because I once had those thoughts, but later I became older and wiser and realized how right he was—on so many things.

Changes have come so gradually that older folks have forgotten much of what life was like back then, and young people have no history to remember unless they've been taught. Some people may have trouble understanding my thinking, so I'll do my best to show how some of my old-fashioned values might need to be the new fashion of today.

I've somehow managed to adapt too much of what is going on in the world. Frankly, I have been pretty successful in keeping up with the times. I try to be modern and sophisticated. But today, some trends are so darned stylish that I feel pushed from my horse and buggy into a Lamborghini.

For Better or Worse

At times, I'm not easily pushed. I still cling to many of my old-fashioned ideas and values.

I am pretty sure that right now there are a lot of people who will disagree with many (maybe most) of the opinions expressed in my essays. If that happens to be you, please be patient, because I respect your right to make your own judgments.

You will never see me among the PC police, because being politically correct isn't what is most important. Instead of rewriting the history book to erase past wrongs, we need to know all the good and bad aspects of history. Only then can we repeat and build on the good while avoiding the bad.

WARNING:

The views and opinions expressed in this book are those of the author and do not necessarily reflect the official policy or position of modern society or any government or political agency.

I don't want anyone to be offended, but if we're too asleep to recognize what's going on, it's time we woke up. Some people get offended at the most trivial things while at the same time ignoring what's really important. This is nothing new. Jesus recognized that problem two thousand years ago when he accused the Pharisees and teachers of the Law of "choking on a gnat but swallowing a camel" (Matthew 23:24).

God knows I have plenty of faults, so I don't want to come across as some self-righteous hypocrite. In fact, I've even been caught not heeding my own advice. We all need reminders if we are to keep getting better.

Many of my lessons have come the hard way. God has very high standards. I have learned how important it is to heed the mental whisper that tells me I might be going the wrong way.

Compass Check

Our values form over many years. Tough situations force choices we don't want to make, and the results aren't always what we expect. Some teach costly lessons that tell us we should check our moral compass and get on the right path.

In my old-fashioned way, I'm challenging you to occasionally check your compass to be sure you're where you want to be. Or maybe this book will make it possible to help a friend who has gone astray.

— Jack Bush

Table of Contents

Why I'm Old-Fashioned

Remember the former things, those of long ago;
I am God, and there is no other; I am God,
and there is none like me. — Isaiah 46:9

My values weren't acquired by accident. Some came with a force that makes me think God was trying to tell me something, if I would only listen. My painful lessons shaped my values with life-saving truth. I hope my experiences will help others without their having to endure such pain.

Changing Times

A ten-cent loaf of bread in the 1930s cost twenty cents in the 1940s and thirty cents in the 1950s. Prices and wages aren't all that have changed in the last eighty years. A lot of our time used to be spent reading, learning, and sharing ideas. Now we spend more time watching television, playing video games, and using our phones for "social" networking. Before we had gated communities, privacy fences, and closed, air-conditioned homes, people spent more time outside, visiting with friends and neighbors.

If you lived as far back as the 1950s, you might remember enough to have some idea what I'm talking about. But most high school and college students can't imagine what it was like. They learned keyboarding, not how to read and write cursive. They don't know what it's like to "dial" a phone or talk on a party line. They seldom enjoy a family meal with everyone at home, and they never gather in the evening to listen to a radio show.

In ancient times, the wisdom of elders was highly respected. A hundred years ago, three generations might live in the same farmhouse. Boys and girls grew up learning from parents and

1

grandparents. But now, parents are often viewed as out-of-touch with the times and grandparents are appreciated mostly for their gifts.

I wonder what people see when I walk by. An old man from the dark ages of ignorance, perhaps. Someone who doesn't understand that modern times are the new, better way. If that's what they think, they probably have never had what I know we've lost—values that matter. They have no clue what parts of the old might make the new so much better.

Lest you think I'm some old grouch who isn't sophisticated enough to understand the realities of today's world, you should know that the values I followed over the years made me highly successful in the modern business world.

Born in a Log Cabin

I was born in a little tenant house in northwest Missouri, during the worst depression in our country's history, when most people in the cities were out of work and starving. On the farm, we might not find anyone to buy the food, but at least we didn't starve.

The government didn't measure the poverty levels in Skidmore, Missouri. Yes, Skidmore really is a town on the map, a farming community first settled in the 1840s. It's still a small town of less than 300 residents. In the 1930s, nobody cared about minimum wage. People worked for whatever someone would pay, and they felt really lucky to get a dime to buy a loaf of bread.

The Less-than-Normal Childhood

When I was eight years old, my parents divorced, which was unusual. In those days, most families stayed together for various reasons, some of which aren't that important in society today. Back then, "till death do us part" really meant something. A couple remained faithful out of love, commitment, religious persuasion, or economic necessity. Whatever the reason, the relationship problems that always exist had to be worked out.

Nevertheless, my parents went their separate ways. I went to live with my grandparents on a farm near King City, about fifty miles away. In this small Missouri town, I was the only kid without a mother and father.

During the depression, most farmers couldn't pay their debts, but my grandparents were frugal, hardworking, and honest. By today's standards, they should have declared bankruptcy, but their old-fashioned moral compasses wouldn't let them default on their obligations. The gigantic debt on their farm was eventually paid off.

Something for Nothing

Financial assistance was available to farmers, but my old-fashioned grandparents weren't willing to take money from the government. If someone offered my grandfather something for nothing, he was always suspicious, a perspective that must have shaped my values as I was growing up. When presented with an "opportunity of a lifetime," a deal that seemed too good to be true, my suspicions led me to discover the truth. Great value comes at high cost. You don't get something for nothing.

My grandparents worked hard, and they expected the same from me. W-O-R-K. Many people today dislike that four-letter word. They think employment means showing up for work, and not necessarily on time. They don't realize that they must work hard and deliver a value in serving customers, or there's no sales income to justify their pay.

When I was growing up, good work was something to be proud of. Doing just enough to get by would be embarrassing. Some people today don't want to work harder until after they are paid more. But no, I needed to work harder and smarter to prove to my boss that I was worth more.

Earn your keep. Always do your best. Don't spend more than you make. Don't do anything you might be ashamed of, because God will know, even if nobody else does. Those values served me well over the ears. And I even had to eat everything on my plate— *before* dessert.

In my eighty-plus years, everything valuable came at significant cost. Even retirement had to be earned through many tough years of hard work. I couldn't expect something for nothing. But now that I am older, I must say that the AARP discounts have been nice.

Child Labor

In the 1930s, everyone old enough to walk was expected to do chores.

By the time I was ten years old, I was earning enough to cover my personal expenses and add to my savings account. Having to work didn't leave me feeling deprived, because that's what most youngsters did. Many worked out of dire necessity, but it was also a social expectation and privilege. We saw ourselves as growing up, gaining confidence that we would one day make it on our own.

By the time I was fourteen, I had a nice little account balance at the bank. I felt very good about that. Saving and investing my money taught me financial responsibility and the value of work.

Today, people who expect to play unless they just *have* to work would find that attitude strange and old-fashioned.

The Right Thing

Some of my values came from living in a small town. I couldn't get away with anything, because everyone in town would soon know. Besides that, God knew, even when I didn't know he knew.

If we were fully aware of God's presence, we might feel like we were driving down the road with a police car behind us, ready to turn on its flashing lights. But after a while, we would get used to doing what was right all the time.

Almost every Sunday, I went to church no matter what. I wasn't super-religious or anything like that. Where I lived, church attendance was what the community expected. Not going to church would have made me stand out as someone odd, and no teenager wanted that.

Most of our residents were dirt poor, but there were no protests or marches about life being unfair. Welfare was seen as our responsibility, not the government's, so we had no reason to protest.

"Sweetie" Miller, the local sheriff, was a strong advocate of law and order. He wouldn't allow anyone to disrupt his quiet little town. He accepted no smart-ass back talking or excuses from lawbreakers acting as if they were deprived and it wasn't their fault.

In King City, you were expected to always do the "right thing," and so just about everybody did. I knew, if I didn't, the news was sure to get back to my grandparents.

Getting to Know God

Blessed is the one . . . whose delight is in the law of the Lord,
and who meditates on his law day and night. — *Psalm 1:1–2*

Going to church was something like checking my rearview mirror.
Otherwise, I wouldn't have known God was watching, and the
rules for good behavior wouldn't have been as important. I soon
learned that it was a good idea to have God on my side by doing
what pleased him.

Praying Well

Some people think prayer is a means for getting what they want. I
saw it more like a chance to talk to God and understand what he
wanted. We can't know people if we don't talk to them, and with
God, that's especially true. It also helps to listen.

In Sunday school classes, I had to memorize Bible verses well
enough to recite them. In King City you were expected to know
quite a bit about God and the Bible. Without an ability to quote an
appropriate Bible verse, I couldn't be a respected part of many
community conversations. Today, an appropriate Bible verse is
hard to find, because so many people don't view Scripture as
absolute truth.

Jesus' Love

Anna Bartlett Warner wrote "Jesus Loves Me" as a poem in 1860,
and it soon became a popular church song among children across
the country. "Jesus loves me—this I know," we sang, "for the Bible
tells me so."

Because we believed Scripture when I was young, I readily accepted the truth of Jesus' love. I believed that truth and got to experience its reality.

Those who are looking for proof outside the Bible will never find it, because they're looking in the wrong place. Jesus loves us, not just because he says so, but because all the stories in the Bible give us reason to believe because they show his love in action.

The Golden Rule

In church, I learned a lot about Jesus' values from what he said and did. How should I treat others? The same way I wanted them to treat me. If I treated them with kindness, even when I was inclined to take offense, odds were good that they would decide to be kind to me.

Today, many say they'll treat others with kindness as soon as they show more kindness. Answering a person's wrong with another wrong is like fighting a fire with gasoline instead of water. We do well to remember the old-fashioned saying that two "wrongs" don't make a "right."

God's Compass

Following what society says is right is like checking a compass with a broken needle. Even if you happen to be going the right way, you have no way to know for sure.

I was fortunate to grow up in a Christian culture that followed a biblical definition of right and wrong. When in doubt, I had to check what God had to say, because I could depend on his word being right, even if I didn't like it.

In our little town there were no such things as "situation ethics" or a "neglected childhood" to hide behind. If I did something wrong, my grandparents would hear about it by the next day.

There was no excuse. I never got away with whining or blaming someone else. I was usually a fast learner, but in this case I wasn't fast enough. Eventually, I understood I could save myself a lot of pain and suffering by always doing what I knew was right.

Feelings of Accomplishment

Well done, good and faithful servant! You have been faithful
with a few things; I will put you in charge of many things.
Come and share your master's happiness! — Matthew 25:23

Everybody has unique, God-given talents in which we should excel.
I'm a bit old-fashioned to recognize that. Many people today think
we should all be alike, and that's a bad mistake.

Valedictorian of My Class

The values I learned at church and from my parents taught me to
do my best. That didn't make me better than everybody else. In my
small high school, others might have been smarter or faster. But
being recognized for my effort always felt good.

To be valedictorian, I had to pay attention in class, do my
homework, and study hard, but I was named captain of the football
team for a different reason. I was willing to be a leader, helping
others. It wasn't because I made good grades.

We don't seem to recognize excellence like we used to. When
everybody gets a trophy and is named a winner, nobody has to try
that hard. I like the old-fashioned way where real winners felt the
joy of victory and losers knew the agony of defeat. No matter
which side I was on, I wanted to do better.

Seeing my name in the Tri-County News was like getting the
gold medal at the end of the race. It made me want to keep
running. But when I wasn't recognized, that was okay. I knew when
I had done well. I also knew I could do better.

A Place for Higher Learning

After high school, I attended the University of Missouri.

By today's standards, our community lived beneath the poverty level. Most of my classmates couldn't afford the cost for attending college. In those days, $1,000 would pay for a year of college, which doesn't sound like much unless you barely have enough to put food on the table. Then it might as well be a million.

High school graduates didn't feel entitled to a college education. They didn't riot or protest. Several went to trade schools or did apprenticeships. Others inherited the responsibility of running the farm.

Fortunately, I had saved money for college and was willing to work hard to help pay my way. After the first year, I dropped out because I thought I already knew enough to be successful in the business world.

I soon found out that I was not nearly as smart as I had thought.

Serving Your Country

President John F. Kennedy is known for saying, "Ask not what your country can do for you. Ask what you can do for our country?" He said those words at a time when attitudes were changing. More and more people were looking for the country to do something for them.

I lived in a day when everyone had a "service obligation." All men eighteen and older had to register for the draft and could look forward to twelve months of active duty or thirty-six months in the reserves. My values compass registered a surge of old-fashioned patriotism.

At age eighteen I enlisted as an Airman Basic in the Air Force National Guard while it was still on active duty. I stayed in for sixteen years altogether, which took work and sacrifice. But it was the right thing to do. I eventually worked up to the rank of captain.

Dodging military service was then considered about as lowdown ornery as any man could get. Patriotism was considered a very good value. In fact, it was an almost mandatory value. I don't recall anyone skipping off to Canada or anything like that then. Those times came later.

Need for Advancement

Family responsibilities led to desires I couldn't fulfill without more education.

When I went back to college, I was married with a baby and very little money. My wife and I used our meager savings and lots of hard work to pay for all our expenses. No financial aid. No food stamps. No welfare. We were on our own, which may be old-fashioned, but it sure made us treasure our education.

Asking for a loan was never considered. Credit is a modern concept that didn't exist in those days. If I had asked First State Bank for a loan, they would have looked at me like I belonged in the mental institutions thirty miles down the road.

When times were tough, as they were most of the time, we just dug in and worked harder. We took on another job. Or we spent less. Ten dollars a week paid for groceries for a family of three, and we couldn't afford to eat out like so many people do today. Instead, we enjoyed family time at home. What a novel idea.

We learned the hard way about getting ourselves educated. We also learned that we didn't like being poor.

I felt fortunate to get a college education. My father had no education at all. He could neither read nor write. College was a big step up for my family.

The American Dream

I believed in the "American Dream," which was different from the modern concept of entitlement. I may be old-fashioned now, but back then I was among a "normal" people who anticipated good fortune as a result of hard work.

With that spirit, I worked my way up from cleaning out manure in barns to being president of some rather large companies. Being company president was a lot better than shoveling manure—most of the time.

Hard work is important, but there is another crucial value that I learned from my Bible. The best way to fulfill the American Dream is to work hard to help others fulfill their dreams. This is different from being the boss who demands performance from others. In part, I became the boss because I felt a great responsibility to help others perform. Do you see the difference?

Many of my dreams came true because I helped a lot of other people's dreams come true. I still firmly believe in the American Dream. It just needs to be the right one.

Hindsight

My wife and I have lived in fourteen different cities and enjoyed the church environment in each one. We have traveled to at least sixty countries. I've lost count of all the governing boards where I've served, from big business to small ministries.

It's not that my wife and I are super-intelligent or the top authorities on anything. We've accomplished so much by making the most of situations by being able and willing to help.

We have had a lot of ups and downs. I'm sorry that so many people today think it shouldn't be that way, because that's the way life is. If they would accept that instead of wasting their energy on complaining, they'd be in a much better position to make their lives better.

If hard times build character and strength, our faces should appear on magazine covers as superheroes. But actually, had it not been for the old-fashioned Christian values we learned to live, those hard times could have just as easily brought our destruction.

We've been dirt poor, lost a child, and faced major death-threatening illnesses. In suffering job losses, we could have spiraled down in failure, but in trusting the Lord we anticipated greater things ahead.

For the last thirty years, I've carried Robert Schuller's "Possibility Thinker's Creed" in my billfold to remind me that anything is possible as I continue to walk with God. Facing a mountain, I'll find a way to climb over, pass through, or tunnel underneath. On the other side of that effort, I'll find a gold mine.

The Bible is an ancient document, but the truth stands forever. It should never get old. I'm living proof that the apostle Paul was stating an absolute reality when he said, "In all things, God works for the good of those who love him, who have been called according to his purpose" (Romans 8:28).

Bigger than All My Problems

Do not fear, for I am with you; do not be dismayed, for I am your God. I will strengthen you and help you; I will uphold you with my righteous right hand. — Isaiah 41:10

God is great. God is good. Let us thank him for our food. That's an old-fashioned saying that today's society should take to heart. When people deny his existence, they deprive themselves of his goodness.

God's Good Side

Without a doubt, God has helped and strengthened me every time I have called on him.

We should value being on God's good side. I could never have made it on my own. All I have accomplished has been with his help.

Priceless Support

God's direction is more than advice. Some have noted that the Ten Commandments weren't called the Ten Suggestions. Nevertheless, we do have a choice. As powerful as God is, we still can ignore his precepts and go our own way.

When I was young, most people knew that wasn't smart. If we get our way, we've cheated ourselves out of a much greater blessing in having what God wants.

Centuries-Old Values

After Jesus ascended into Heaven, his apostles and disciples spread the gospel message. Initially, people called "Christian" were being ridiculed, as if only ignorant people would ever act like Jesus, helping the helpless and loving the unlovable.

People who hated the message persecuted and killed the messengers. God's faithful followers were beaten, crucified, and burned alive. Before cheering crowds, they were torn apart by wild animals in the arenas. Like lambs led to slaughter, they didn't fight back but continued to declare their faith, even when it cost their lives. We might call them "Roaring Lambs."

When the apostle Paul was killed in the first century, the number of committed Christians scattered across the Roman Empire might have been less than three thousand. But some three hundred years later, that number had soared into the tens of millions. Why? God's values became so important that they became the law of the land.

Roaring Faith

Without the persecution, the values that were once so important can be easily forgotten. As the apostle Paul once wrote, some people will have a "form of godliness" (2 Timothy 3:5) but deny its power. For two centuries, America was been known as a Christian nation, but not so much anymore. Why? Many who call themselves Christian have become more concerned with appearing righteous, following the form, but they ignore the values that were taught in the first century.

We need to become Roaring Lambs again.

Practicing What You Preach

Perhaps you've noticed that some unbelievers follow God's values better than some Christians. I personally don't care what the religion or creed is, as long as the values of faith, hope, and love are followed. Don't you suppose people who do that are more likely to find eternal life in Christ than those who profess a relationship with God but don't follow his principles? I think so.

Being old-fashioned, I'm more concerned with who I am on the inside than how I look on the outside. I care more about what God thinks of me than what others think, so I don't mind letting people know I love God and seek to please him.

Every day, I thank God for being so good to me, helping me live better. If people will see how my old-fashioned values have blessed me, maybe they will choose to follow the Lord and enjoy the more abundant life that Jesus offers.

Changing Times

*You must no longer live as the Gentiles . . . darkened
in their understanding and separated from the life of God
because of the ignorance that is in them due to the
hardening of their hearts. — Ephesians 4:17–18*

Maybe being old-fashioned can come back into style. I'm not looking for a return of double-breasted suits and wide ties. We don't need petticoats and pantyhose. The changes we need are a return to values that make life better.

Old-Fashioned Relic

Some kind of ad campaign seems to be going in which God is likened to a person who was important for people in horse-and-buggy days, but not for the educated geniuses graduating from our universities today. If so, we've become too smart for our own good.

Public prayer has become shameful, something that should never be seen, lest it offend someone or make them uncomfortable. Popular movies and television shows present marital faithfulness as strange behavior. Christians need to keep their convictions to themselves. If they aren't politically correct, they can face lawsuits and lose their jobs.

Outside the Bible belt across the South, odds are good that someone walking down the street couldn't correctly guess the names of the four gospels. Where was Jesus born? What was his profession? Most people don't know, which tells us how unimportant Jesus and his message have become.

Christianity under Attack

News articles have challenged people to re-think their faith in Christ as if such beliefs aren't realistic. In a local newspaper, I saw a two-page article that said the old ideas about Heaven and Hell couldn't possibly be correct. Do you get the picture here? Christians should keep quiet about their values, but everyone else is allowed free speech.

I wonder what God thinks of the sophisticated independent thinkers who don't value God or his principles. I can guess. The Bible gives several examples of God's judgment in the Old Testament. So why doesn't he punish all the evil people who won't listen to him? That day will come, maybe in our lifetime. But for now, according to one apostle, God is waiting for more people to see the error of their ways and turn to him (2 Peter 3:9).

People who spend a lot of time watching national news will enjoy a steady diet of tragedy and injustice. You might see headlines that say, "God Isn't Fixing This" or "Where Is God When You Need Him?" You may hear radio and television hosts ridicule those who say they talk to God. Whose values do you think are better?

The hosts obviously like their views, perhaps because they appeal to their audiences, boost ratings, and make them money. But what about the viewers?

How much might a host's anti-Christ views sway the conviction of people who are watching? I think the answer might be found in how much time people spend watching television versus the time spent in church.

The values we cultivate and water are the values that will grow.

What's Happening

The bad-mouthing of someone else's religion seems to be fashionable among the social elite, and it's nothing new. It's been happening for thousands of years. It's the "I'm right and therefore everybody else has to be wrong" syndrome. Some Christians have that view, but I still don't like it.

God gave people the free will to choose their values, whether they will hear and follow him or go their own self-serving way. As much as I would *like* to turn people's values to the Lord, I can't. If

16

they want to believe a lie, they can make that lie their "truth," and they can call God's truth a "lie."

Bad-mouthing someone's religion is a good idea only if your goal is to feel better about yourself. It won't help others. It will make them defensive, damage relationships, and strengthen their beliefs.

The Double Standard

In my day, we called this "the pot calling the kettle black." Jesus chided people for pointing at a speck in someone's eye when they had something much bigger in their own (Matthew 7:4–5). This seems to point to a common aspect of human nature that we see other people's faults more easily than our own.

Years ago, we had a saying: "It takes one to know one." I've learned to be careful about accusing people, because having a fault myself might be the reason I so quickly recognize it in others. If that's true, then Jesus was right. I need God's help in fixing my issues, and then I'll be in a position to help others, not accuse them.

A Reign of Terror

Christianity is unique in its message that God will walk with us to help the helpless and love the unlovable, including our enemies. Other religions exclude outsiders, and some seek to kill the infidels who refuse to believe like they do. Do you get the picture? We should love others, but that doesn't mean they will always respond with kindness. They might want to cut your head off.

With my old-fashioned values of trusting God, I didn't have to worry about what others might do in response to my doing what was right. I should be more concerned about how God would feel in response to my doing what was wrong.

But today, in the age of political correctness, we tend to be more concerned about what people think than we are about what God wants. When that value infiltrates Christian belief, we put ourselves under terror for what others might think about us or do to us.

We need to fear God more than we fear the terrorists.

Changing Society

Survey the right people and ask the right questions, and you can get statistics to support just about anything you want to believe. For me, the numbers don't matter as much as what I see in the world around me. To be hired, university professors of religion need to be agnostic. In churches, we hear more about God's forgiveness than the importance of a sin-free life.

In my early church days, people carried their Bibles to services and read them at home. Not anymore. Now, the only scripture they read is what they might see on the screen during a weekend message. They no longer carry their Bibles. I see people holding their cell phones in church, but I'm not certain whether they are reading a verse or something on the Internet.

In the old days, people might not go to church, but they didn't question God's existence. During World War II, we knew there were no unbelievers in the fox holes, where bullets were flying over soldiers' heads. Now, we find people everywhere who aren't sure God exists, even in the fox holes. A soldier could be in trouble if he leaves a Bible where it might be seen. A large percentage of those who go to church do so out of convenience, not commitment.

With these trends, some preach doom and gloom while others predict a great revival. Who is right? The book of Revelation doesn't paint a pretty picture of the future, but with my old-fashioned values, I don't have to worry—as long as if I'm on God's side. Dismal as the future might be for most people, Revelation makes it clear that God will take care of those who seek to please him.

The way I see it, "Faith is not about everything turning out okay. Faith is about being okay, no matter how things turn out."

More than Just Believing

Trust in the Lord with all your heart and lean not on your
own understanding; in all your ways submit to him, and he
will make your paths straight. — Proverbs 3:5

The Bible says the devils believe and tremble (James 2:19), so
saying we believe God exists and Jesus is God's son isn't enough.
Faith believes in the rewards for doing what God wants, no matter
what it costs (Hebrews 11:6).

Faith in Action

Faith in God helped me be a better person, and that made me a
better husband, father, and grandfather. Those old-fashioned values
of love and faithfulness made a better marriage. With God's help,
we made it through the tough times and learned to appreciate his
gifts. Take away those values, and our marriage might have wound
up on the rocks. And I doubt that I would ever have been
successful in business.

Some people think God will go with them wherever they go.
Maybe so, but after Jonah spent three days in the belly of a fish, I
think he'd say it's a much better idea to go where God wants. The
Bible says two can't walk together unless they have agreed to do so
(Amos 3:3). My old-fashioned values say it's a lot better to agree
with God and go where he leads.

Perhaps because I took that approach, God just keeps hanging
in there with us. He comforts us in our old age, with countless
pleasure-filled memories of his goodness. The Holy Spirit has been
there for us when we most needed him.

God may not always answer prayers the way I want, but my old-
fashioned faith says that what God wants is always better in the

end. His plan is better than anything I could put together. Therefore, prayer has been and always will be a huge part of our lives

Our Best Friend

Exposing how we really feel could change what others think of us. If people knew our faults and failures, relationships could be damaged beyond repair. Knowing that, we try to control our behavior—until our emotions get the best of us.

Here's the wonderful thing about God: nothing is hidden from him. He even knows the secrets I've hidden from myself because I don't want to face them. And he *still* loves me.

God won't be upset if I tell him how I really feel. I can be open and honest with him. He won't be offended or think less of me if I admit my weaknesses, express my concerns, and expose my emotions to him. When I need to talk to someone about life's problems and opportunities, he's right there, listening, wanting the best for me.

I highly recommend that your values include having a good and long-lasting relationship with God and that you talk with him often.

Trusted Resource

An old-fashioned message is still printed on our money: "In God we trust." Some people today would like to see those words removed, because they trust their money more than they trust God.

Over the years, I've come to know God better. He's caused bad things to work together for good. I found hope in him when failure seemed unavoidable. I've learned that money is as easily lost as it's gained. God is the one to be trusted, because he continues to turn tragedies into triumphs. How can I be quiet about that?

Born to Roar

I wish more people in our country would speak up and praise God for being good. Jesus' disciples said the news was too good to be kept secret, that they had to tell what they had seen and heard (Acts 4:20). Years ago, we had fiery preachers in tent-meeting revivals, where people came early or they might not find a seat. People were so excited about their newfound relationships with Christ that they just had to tell their friends. Why have those values changed?

Maybe we've hidden our treasure like diamonds locked in a safe. If so, we should renew the thrill we once had, like the bride who wants everyone to see her ring and share her joy. How do we do that?

When my wife and I became members of the Roaring Lambs Bible Study, I got a fresh look at the richness and beauty of God's gifts. My faith is amplified as I'm reminded of God's goodness. With renewed excitement, I want others to have this treasure too. I can't keep quiet. For as long as I have breath, I need to roar.

Snakes and Doves

As I refer to "roaring," I'm talking about not being timid. Instead, we openly express our convictions to *help* people, not scare them away. That's the difference between a roaring lion and a roaring lamb.

The apostle Paul told Christians to "season their messages with salt" (Colossians 4:6). In other words, we should do our best to make what we're serving appetizing, which is what Paul did when he referred to the Athenians' monument to "the unknown God" and quoted their ancient poet Epimenides with "in him we live and move and have our being" (Acts 17:23–28).

People have many beliefs, and they are all to be respected in their right to embrace whatever religion they choose. No matter what we believe, we must all give up misconceptions before we can get to know the one true God better. We're not likely to do that when we feel threatened.

When Jesus sent disciples into the Judean country to preach the Kingdom of God, he told them to be "wise as serpents and harmless as doves" (Matthew 10:16). What did he mean by that? In ancient homes, snakes could slip through cracks, unnoticed. Unlike other birds, doves flee when threatened. They do not defend their nests. So we slip in, unnoticed, eager to give an answer for the hope we have in Christ (1 Peter 3:15), but if people reject the way we tell the story, defending our faith won't change their minds. We should leave.

Resisting Radicals

I do have big-time problems with radical extremists who want to kill those who don't believe like they do. Whether we are liberal or conservative, Democrat or Republican, protestant or Catholic, Islamist or Jew, the radical religious don't follow the old-fashioned practice of treating others like we want to be treated.

The not-so-golden rule today seems to say, "I might treat others with kindness, but only if they are kind to me and agree with me." I sincerely question their values and whether they will enjoy the "paradise" they anticipate.

If we love our enemies, as Jesus said we should do, we won't attack them, but we should be like his disciples who feared God more than people and declared his truth, no matter the cost.

A Time of Crisis

People will be . . . unforgiving, slanderous, without self-control
. . . lovers of pleasure rather than lovers of God—having a
form of godliness but denying its power. — 2 Timothy 3:2–5

In just the last thirty years, I have seen drastic changes in our relationships with one another. Marriage and family values aren't what they used to be. What we once called "cursing like a sailor" is mild compared to the graphic language people might hear at work today. Gunfights that were once reserved for the O.K. Corral have moved to concerts, schools, and churches. Can there be any doubt that America is facing a values crisis?

Those who want freedom from religion are working harder than ever to put God and faith out of the American way of life. As graphic violence and sex has become more acceptable in the media, similar behavior becomes the norm at home and at work. The seriousness of the situation cannot be overstated.

I've heard church leaders say we now face the greatest confrontation in history between the Gospel and the anti-Gospel, between Christ and those who oppose Christ. What was seen in the first century (1 John 2:18) may be nothing compared to where we're headed today.

Fifty years ago, denying prayer at public events was unthinkable. Display of crosses, the Ten Commandments, and Christmas nativity scenes were never questioned. To do so back then would have been a public offense. But now, we are most concerned about not offending just one atheist or agnostic.

Might of the Media

With the growth of the Internet, streaming movies, and the ability to view video electronic devices everywhere, the mass media now exerts much greater influence on our values. What was once known to be sinful is now glamorized. Faith in God might be questioned or ridiculed as absurd and outdated. I wonder how much longer Christians will be able to stand up for biblical principles and not be accused of hate speech.

What is driving the anti-God sentiment? Perhaps it could be summarized in the single phrase: "the love of money," which the apostle Paul said was the root of all evil (1 Timothy 6:10). For higher ratings and to make more money, the media caters to the audience's insatiable desire for pleasure.

As hard as the media tries, though, I won't change my old-fashioned Bible-thumping values that have made my life more satisfying than many can imagine.

The New Face of Religion

If the apostle Paul were to walk into church today, I wonder what he would say. Our gatherings have little in common with what existed in the first century.

In the last thirty years, worship in an increasing number of churches has moved from a song leader accompanied by piano or organ to a band and vocalists who fill the stage. In some cases, few people are singing. Most are just listening. The preaching seems to have changed too—from biblically based teaching to philosophical messages of encouragement.

The churches described in the Bible had traits that God condemned (Revelation 2–3). Many people abandoned their passion for God while some stood strong when facing persecution. Some embraced false teaching and the pursuit of fleshly pleasures. Churches that claimed to be alive were actually dead. Saying they were rich, they were actually poor, having a religious form without much of the Holy Spirit at work.

We would do well to heed the message John gave to the churches in the book of Revelation. While a popular message may draw big crowds, I wonder if what we call "strength" is actually a

24

"weakness," offering a superficial feeling of wellbeing without doing much to calm the raging storms hidden in people's hearts.

Along the way, my wife and I have been members of some great churches. And some were not so great. For me, the winners were not ashamed of old-fashioned biblical values. Preaching didn't cater to political correctness at every new twist of society.

When Things Get Tough

Hall-of-Fame quarterback and Coach Knute Rockne is credited with saying, "When things get tough, the tough get going." Great idea, but exactly how do the tough do that when they don't have the strength?

When things get really tough, like what my wife and I have been through

- being out of work and without a job,
- losing a child,
- surviving six cancers,
- or facing my almost deadly Wegener's Disease, what could I do but trust the Lord?

Without our old-fashioned trust in God when people thought there was no hope, without the work of the Holy Spirit, our toughness would never have been enough. When things got tough—like with the loss of a child—we wisely turned to the Lord for strength.

A few years ago, I was standing at death's door, given only two or three days to live. When the family had been called to say their goodbyes, I didn't want to hear a prayer and be told everything would be all right. I needed a serious talk with God. Mayo Clinic helped save my life, but the Holy Spirit gave me the hope, faith, and strength to live.

The same was true for my wife. Her famous oncologist at the Mayo Clinic said, "It is not unusual for people to have six cancers, but it is very unusual for them to still be alive." Without the work of the Holy Spirit, the work of the Mayo Clinic wouldn't have been enough to extend her life for more than twenty-five years, so far. We can thank the doctors, but the greater praise belongs to God.

Unexplainable Peace

The Bible describes a time when Jesus' disciples were terrified, sure they were about to drown, and Jesus was asleep in the boat (Mark 4:37–40). After speaking to the wind and waves, calming the storm, Jesus said they didn't have to be afraid. Why?

People may see the turmoil around us and can't understand how we can be at peace. The answer is having Jesus in our boat and knowing that living or dying doesn't matter as long as we're with him. That old-fashioned trust in God that everything will be all right is the only way to have true peace of mind.

I don't know how to define Hell, but I see it as something more painful than physical fire and brimstone. Many people, including Christians, don't want to believe Hell exists, but that doesn't do much to calm their fear of dying. I think people who make excuses for wrongdoing wind up experiencing a taste of Hell on Earth, because they haven't fully surrendered their lives to Christ. If they knew he was in their boat, they might enjoy a taste of Heaven instead.

Identity Theft

Changing the label doesn't change the nature of the fruit or the tree where it came from. Believing something is good will not cause sour fruit to be sweet. Much is said today about the importance of positive thinking, as if declaring something good will make it good.

People may smile and say, "I love you," but their actions reveal their true identity. Jesus said, just as we can identify a tree by its fruit, people's actions reveal their true identity (Matthew 7:20).

My old-fashioned values say I should be most concerned about who I am on the inside and place less importance on how I look on the outside. Looking good is a poor substitute for *being* good, and for that, I've needed God's help.

People whose hope is in God will find strength. "They will soar on wings like eagles. They will run and not grow weary. They will walk and not be faint" (Isaiah 40:31).

Horse and Carriage

A man will leave his father and mother and be united to his wife . . . no longer two, but one . . . What God has joined together, let no one separate. — Mark 10:7–9

For some things to function at their best, they need to be together—like a horse and carriage. A chariot without wheels, an airplane without wings, or a boat without a rudder is useless.

Love and Marriage

Every night, I thank God that I found the right person to share my life with. We were high school sweethearts, who married in our late teens. In those days when kids learned to do chores as soon as they could walk, teenagers quickly learned adult responsibilities and often married before they were twenty.

After over sixty-five years of marriage, my wife and I are still sweethearts, very much in love. Like a horse and carriage, marriage needs love. If we hadn't made that old-fashioned commitment, "till death do us part," I doubt whether we could have made it down life's bumpy roads.

In the old days, marriage was a lifetime commitment, and divorce was cause for embarrassment. But today, marriage is often a convenience until something better comes along. Fewer divorces only means that more couples are living together without getting married. We've made divorce acceptable and convenient, because life's inevitable conflicts cannot be resolved without love.

Today, you can be married without living together. Or you can live together without being married. Just about any lifestyle seems acceptable as long as it feels good. Children may be left to their grandparents or to government-assigned foster care.

Mr. or Miss Right

Dating services have never been more popular, but in the old-fashioned days, we had a better way. We had church and school functions where groups enjoyed life together. Inner beauty was valued more than sex appeal. We got to know one another in everyday life, which is much more important than what happens in the bedroom.

People who think they've found their sleeping beauty or knight in shining armor need only face a major difficulty to see how wrong their expectations were. Marriage isn't a 50–50 commitment. It's a need for 100 percent caring by each partner, no matter what the conditions are.

When my wife and I said our wedding vows, each phrase—to love, honor and cherish . . . in sickness and health . . . to have and to hold—meant something. Those were promises made for the worst as well as the best of times.

After hearing how long we've been married, people will often say, "Wow! What's your secret?" as if marriage for a lifetime is some kind of miracle. Too many people think love is a warm, fuzzy feeling. But actually, love that endures is a cold, hard commitment to fight life's challenges together and never make war with each other to get our own way.

Forgotten Virtue

Many have forgotten that patience is a virtue. Don't think your influence will change your spouse overnight. Maybe a little after ten years. More after twenty-five. A couple must walk together for decades, seeking to agree and agreeing to disagree until they eventually become as one in thought and purpose.

Patience allows us to be grateful for our unique strengths, which allow us to cover for each other's weaknesses. As we do that, neither of us would want to live without the other. I wish those old-fashioned values were more active today.

Different but Alike

Today's compatibility values are pursuing impossibilities.

No couple begins a relationship with the same desires. In fact, every man and woman is different. No two people are the same. If two people were exactly alike, they wouldn't be compatible. Since no two people are ever alike, the best thing we can do is accept our differences, like two pieces of a picture puzzle that wouldn't fit together if they were alike.

My wife and I are very different, yet we are very much alike. Our minds don't work the same way. I look for a logical solution while she's more concerned with what feels right. Our abilities and skills are different. But one crucial area where we are alike is in our values. If both of us hadn't stood for strong Christian values, I doubt we would have survived many dates, let alone get married.

Because of that secure foundation, old-fashioned as it was, we have been able to share our goals and see the fulfillment of many dreams, living together in a pretty unselfish way.

Hard Work

My wife and I are both old-fashioned in another respect, I think. Good fortune is *earned* with hard work. That's especially true in marriage.

Today, many people marry for "the good life," as if love should come without struggles. Expecting marriage to give them everything they want, they are soon disappointed, seek pleasures elsewhere, and wind up in divorce.

Love is a commitment to stay together through the tough times. With that resolve, we attacked life's challenges together rather than fighting each other for our way. This was a value that had to be learned through all our ups and downs. It was very hard work.

My mother and father were examples of what *not* to do. Divorced when I was eight years old, they went their separate ways, leaving me to be raised by my grandparents. My parents lacked the patience and persistence that my old-fashioned grandparents demonstrated. If couples understood the tragic effect divorce has on children, they wouldn't be so quick to separate. Had it not been for loving grandparents, I would have drowned in my problems instead of achieving success.

Standing by each other is easy in the good times. The bad times are what really prove our love. Giving up is not an option when true love exists.

The Divorce Culture

Without loving parents, what should we expect? Without love, we have hatred, anger, and all sorts of violence, the kinds of behavior we often see today.

The new norms are dysfunctional, single-parent, and parentless families. Modern television portrays the typical family conditions instead of the loving relationships shown in *Father Knows Best, My Three Sons,* and *Leave It to Beaver* with their old-fashioned values.

Today, we just don't see many television series or movies that promote Christian values. Why? Evidently, such conditions are no longer visualized by the producers as ideal enough to attract big profits from the general audience. Divorce and promiscuous lifestyles are glamorized. Producers may seek an R rating for their movies, because they believe a milder rating would be less profitable.

What would happen if all Christians refused to spend money on anything R-rated and favored faith-based productions? Producers would have to follow the new money trail and create better-quality, wholesome movies.

The Old-Fashioned Carriage

Love is patient . . . kind . . . does not dishonor others . . .
is not self-seeking . . . not easily angered . . . does not
delight in evil but rejoices with the truth.
Love never fails. — 1 Corinthians 13:4–8

Weddings today sometimes include the old-fashioned carriage ride, a symbol of romantic times that are fading from modern reality. Today, marriage is more like shopping for cars until you find the color and make that most suits you.

The Unhitched Style

Many single adults seem to think they should try out different relationships before getting hitched. This "horseless carriage" expects to run on *conditional* love, which is like pushing off down the hill. Everything runs great until the going gets tough. Without the unconditional commitment of marriage, the carriage can't make it through the rough, uphill climb.

Without marriage, what we might call "love" is unhitched from its true meaning of self-sacrifice for the sake of the *other* person. Instead, we have an unhitched love with an insatiable appetite for sex and self-serving pleasures. When one person fails to satisfy, or another person has greater appeal, it's time to move on.

Years ago in my hometown, "getting hitched" meant two people being tied together by marriage. That's much different from what's popular today, when people say, "Let's hook up."

By definition the unhitched style is always in jeopardy, with being "hooked up" as likely to be broken up as to be kept together.

Together Forever

To gain freedom from oppression in Europe, our ancestors had to make a lifetime commitment to leave their homes and endure life threatening hardship in America. Being free from one thing meant becoming slaves to something else.

For as long as single people are unwilling to "settle down," they deprive themselves of the freedom that comes with a lifelong commitment of marriage. They think a "forever" relationship means they would have to give up all the fun they're having. They're right. What they don't realize is that they're depriving themselves of a relationship that is much more rewarding.

When a husband and wife are fully committed to each other, they can enjoy a new kind of fun that is indescribably better. And it lasts forever.

Blessed with Children

The Bible speaks of many children being a blessing (Psalm 127:5), and that was still true when I was young. Large families were common in those days. Not so much anymore.

Today, children are often seen as a curse, not a blessing, which explains why abortion is so common. In the old farming communities, more children meant extra hands to do the chores and keep food on the table. Too often now, they are seen as a hindrance, not a help.

With my old-fashioned values, I get to enjoy the family blessing of children and grandchildren. I'm sorry that so many people today don't know how wonderful a family gathering can be.

Gay Pride

Same-sex marriage has gained amazing popularity in recent years, which is an amazing reversal of social attitudes in just a few decades. What was once detested is now accepted, if not desired, by many. I'm in no position to judge every situation, but I know what the Bible says. The fact that so many want to ignore those verses shows how far society has distanced itself from God's Word.

I find it interesting that gay folks are fighting *for* marriage when so many others are fighting for divorce or to never get married.

What we're seeing is dysfunction everywhere, both in and out of marriage, which is sad. But isn't that what we would expect of society when God is no longer the center of people's lives?

Those who don't believe in God or don't agree with God are sure to go in another direction, with a different set of values.

Since I'm not gay and I'm not inclined that way, I'm in no position to make sense of gay marriage. I've had mentors who were gay. In my professional work life, many of my associates were gay. They were all wonderful, caring people. I wish I could say that was true in my relationship with all the people who called themselves *Christian*.

I wonder what the children will become, when they have two mothers with no father or two fathers with no mother. Perhaps they will struggle, unsure who they are, male or female, or what they want to be in adult life. What about the other children, those who grow up in single-parent families, orphanages, or foster homes? The new way doesn't seem to be working very well.

I still cling to the old-fashioned carriage idea that "marriage" is best defined as between one man and one woman. But before we condemn the LGBTQ community as going-to-hell sinners, we might want to look at ourselves. Besides homosexuality, the Bible condemns drunkenness and overeating. When did we last hear a sermon focusing on those sins? That's not to say one sin justifies another. It's saying that any sin, even those we might want to say is trivial, separates us from God to some degree. We fall short of the glory and abundant life that he wants for us.

Our belief in God is our individual choice. We don't have to believe if we don't want to. But if we believe the truth and surrender our lives to Christian principles, we'll focus on what we need to do that's right, not on condemning others for what we see as wrong.

True Love

I've read studies that say married couples enjoy more physical and emotional happiness than couples that never tie the knot. I don't know how that can be proven, but it makes sense to me. If my wife and I had just "lived together," the lack of an official commitment would have weakened our ability to fight through the tough times together. Going our separate ways was not an option, because we had vowed to stay together "till death do us part." From my personal experience, I have to say the benefits of marriage far outweighed the difficulties.

The romantic feelings that come from courtship and the honeymoon are not what we should call "true love." God showed us true love when he cared for us when we were sinners, loving the unlovable. We demonstrate true love when it's something we give with no hope for anything in return. Husbands love their wives, with or without makeup, and will help with the housework and raising the kids. Wives show love when their husbands are overweight and forget to take out the trash. Both should be more concerned about serving than they are for being served.

When my wife and I were complaining about each other's faults, she often repeated the saying, "Well, you made your bed . . . now lie in it." That was her kind way of saying we had made an irreversible commitment to accept our differences and make the best of them. Complaining wasn't helping.

The old-fashioned carriage called for pulling together.

Hitched Together

Together, my wife and I have been able to achieve financial wellbeing and stability. Neither of us would have been this successful on our own. We comforted each other when things did not go well. There were plenty of disasters in our lives that needed a lot of comforting, or we would have given up.

We faced the challenges of our occupations together, encouraging each other to do our best. Each of us was eager to do whatever we could to help, no matter the cost.

Raising a family was a great delight, because we were together. Since my grandparents had to raise me, I have a good understanding of how tragic our relationships would have been if my wife and I had ever separated.

For kids whose parents are unhitched, love, encouragement, and stability have an entirely different meaning.

My wife and I are now in our "golden years," a time when I have many opportunities to think about what life would have been like without each other. When sickness and major health problems occurred, having "each other" helped us pull through and have hope for the future.

Joys Shared

What a thrill it is to catch a huge fish and release it back into the water. After so many times on the golf course, sinking a hole in one is something every duffer wants to talk about. But I have to say my achievements wouldn't have meant much without a person to share them with.

A lot should be said about having a companion in the ups and downs of life. Dealing with grief is twice as hard when we are alone, and celebrating victories are twice as wonderful when we can share them. I must say, the goodnight kiss every night, the hug first thing every morning, and our conversations during mealtimes are wonderful. When friends and relatives can be included, the joys broaden and add abundance to our lives.

Our contribution to society has been better because of these two words: love and marriage. Without the carriage, the horse would be alone. So I'm thankful for the old-fashioned carriage.

Sweet Land of Opportunity

Forgetting what is behind and straining toward what is ahead,
I press on toward the goal to win the prize for which
God has called me. — Philippians 3:13–14

I believe we live in an exceptional country, unlike anywhere else in the world. Love for the land of the free and the home of the brave is definitely one of my old-fashioned values.

America's Blessing

We still sing about spacious skies and amber waves of grain, but our flag no longer has the widespread respect that it once had. In some settings, people might sing, "God bless America," or "my eyes have seen the coming of the Lord," but those values seem to be fading rapidly.

A shrinking percentage of people know the words to our national anthem, The Star-Spangled Banner. A professional singer at a sports event can mess up what are now less-than-familiar words. Some choose to kneel or in some way show disrespect for our flag and our country. I admire those who will stand and salute, remembering the thousands who died so we could be blessed.

For two centuries, we have valued our "freedom of religion." Churches were respected places of worship, and Christians were regarded as loving, merciful people, always seeking to do what was right. But now, too many are ignoring "IN GOD WE TRUST" on our money and our Pledge of Allegiance that says we are "one nation under God."

As society distances itself from God and emphasis shifts to freedom *from* religion, we're losing touch with the One who has blessed America for so long.

Equal Rights

Our country still offers exceptional opportunities, but we value them differently, more as rights than a possibility to be pursued. The U.S. Declaration of Independence asserts the self-evident truth that "all men are created equal." When those words were written, they objected to social prejudice that said lords were better than peasants, and common people had neither ability nor opportunity for excellence.

The modern concept says we should all be alike. Both men and women should work the same jobs and receive the same pay, having equal value. Both winners and losers should receive a trophy, because we don't want anyone to feel unequal. If we continue on this path and still believe in God, we'll soon be saying that sin doesn't matter. Both saints and sinners will be saved because God loves everyone.

Our Creator didn't make us the same. He made us all different, with unique talents and abilities, each person equipped to fulfill a special purpose. Nobody gets a trophy for being like someone else.

Uniquely Different

We don't need to duplicate the efforts of Thomas Edison, Albert Einstein, or Marie Curie. That work has already been done.

Throughout history, our old-fashioned values have produced exceptional people, exceptional ideas, and exceptional results. If we quit medicating people who think and act differently so they can be like everybody else, we might develop geniuses who dare to be different, people who will achieve what was thought impossible.

Four Freedoms

After the attack on Pearl Harbor in 1941, President Roosevelt gave a speech to Congress, outlining our country's greatest values: freedom of speech, freedom of worship, freedom from want, freedom from fear.

In traveling around the world, I've been able to compare the U.S. to most other countries. I've seen breathtaking scenes and met many wonderful people, but I have yet to find anywhere that has all the freedoms of home. Each trip made me proud to be an American.

Building the Good Life

When I was growing up, my grandparents, teachers, and peers believed in the reward for hard work. Nobody was saying that pursuing our dreams would be easy.

"Build yourself a life," people said. "You can do it. America is a land of endless opportunities." Millions of immigrants arrived in our country, believing their dreams of freedom and opportunity could be true.

Now, I'm afraid we take too much for granted. Either we fail to appreciate what we have, or we complain about what we don't have, as if achieving "the good life" should be easy.

I don't want to minimize the severe obstacles some people face. I remember what it was like to struggle without a paycheck, wondering how I was going to survive. Discrimination is a problem, but that shouldn't be used to justify our own discriminations. The road upward is much more difficult for some than for others. No matter what our status is, we need to strive for better. We should be seeking to serve others rather than protesting when we've not been properly served. It's a bit old-fashioned to say so, but we don't have to allow ourselves to be victims of our circumstances.

Discrimination

Politicians and some news media scream about racism, bigotry, and a long list of other social biases. Of course those things exist. They always have. But the intense focus today tries to paint a picture that America is "unfair." Many colleges and universities seem to be caught up in promoting that idea.

Anybody can think they aren't paid enough for the work they do. They don't get the respect they deserve. They don't get the promotion they've worked so hard for. What they have isn't as much as they ought to have. And to hear them tell it, it's not their fault. They've been discriminated against.

When I talked with God about this, I felt that I needed to "get over that *excuse* stuff." His direction was very clear to me. I can't keep people from sometimes being inconsiderate. I can be ignored or mistreated, but so what? I needed to quit complaining about others doing me wrong, but shift my focus on me to do what's right.

White Privilege

There seems to be a lot of "class warfare" talked up these days. Stones are cast at the so-called rich. Supposedly, elite privilege is why some people have so much. They infer that in a "fair" economic system, less-effective people should get the same rewards as those who work harder, get more education, and are more innovative. I guess that is a value thing . . . for them.

Old-fashioned values recognize that people are not equal in their ambition, determination, and intellect. But no matter how talented we might be, digging out of poverty is not easy. I've been there. The hill is extremely hard to climb, especially if you think life is unfair.

My wife and I were not from so-called "white privileged families," that's for sure. We grew up in a farming community where poverty was the normal way of life. I can show you pictures of the little stone tenant house where I was born. Or the tiny place where my wife and I first lived. In our small one-bedroom apartment, we scraped and saved money, hoping for the day when we could own our own home.

We dreamed we could somehow overcome being poor. We didn't like being poor, and if that was going to change, we would have to make it happen. Blaming others and making excuses wouldn't help. We never visualized how far we could go in this world. It happened because of education and hard work, not privilege.

Rising to the Top

My wife and I thought we could rise up in the world because we lived in America—the land of opportunity. We looked around and saw successful people and said to ourselves, *That picture sure looks a*

39

lot better than being poor and uneducated. I really wanted to do something better than shoveling manure in barns, which was my job early in life.

Does our country have faults? Is our society sometimes unfair? Yes. But those liabilities don't have to keep us from rising to the top—unless we allow them to.

The winding uphill road to the top will have plenty of obstacles to overcome. But the important thing to know is that you can overcome just about anything if you want to badly enough. That seems like a good value to me.

In recent years, I've heard people apologize for the affluence of our country. They seem embarrassed that God could have blessed some people more than others, so they call for "social justice" where the government makes everyone prosperous. Who will pay for this? All those greedy, rich people, of course.

People can live on welfare if they want to, but it's not the rewarding life they can have through education and hard work. There are no helicopter rides to the top. We have to make it the old-fashioned way. We *earn* it.

The Victim Mentality

Many people today see themselves as victims. Why? Perhaps because that's what they've been told so many times that they only see the evidence that points that way. How easily they can be offended or feel abused or underprivileged. It doesn't take much to believe the whole world is at war against them.

As I hear people complain, I have to wonder why they don't flee to another country. There's a reason why so many citizens of other counties want to come to America. This is still a land of opportunity. So we don't have to be victims unless that's what we want to believe.

The Problem with Socialism

I recently saw a survey of how many people said they would vote for a socialist president. I was appalled. Have they quit teaching history in school? No government has ever been good at playing Robin Hood, taking from the rich and giving to the poor. The concept must fail, because we eventually run out of other people's money. And in the process, the "other people" lose their incentive to work so hard. Most rich people don't mind giving, but they don't like seeing their assets stolen, and that's how they feel when the government takes such a big percentage.

My old-fashioned values say we should be cautious when politicians tell us something that sounds too good to be true. We want to believe the charismatic people who tell us what we want to hear. But is it true? Too often, the politicians' words don't match what they actually do.

Patriotic Goosebumps

I must have heard the song 'God Bless America' a thousand times, but I still get the same goosebumps I had in grade school. This nation is still very blessed, and I hope we can learn some old-fashioned values that will keep it that way.

Four-Letter Words

*Whatever is true, whatever is noble . . . right . . . pure . . .
lovely . . . admirable—if anything is excellent or
praiseworthy—think about such things.* — *Philippians 4:8*

With my old-fashioned values, I'm bothered by the dark four-letter
words that express so much bitterness, anger, and perversion—
words that were never heard when I was young. We may bleep the
words on public television and avoid saying them in church, but
they are so commonly used in our culture that everyone knows
what is meant when the two middle letters of four-letter words are
left out in print.

We should focus on the *great* four-letter words that deserve
being spelled out and emphasized.

Work

In recent years, I've known people in the workplace who acted like
they thought *work* was a curse word. When I was a kid, I thought
work was fun. My, how values have changed.

When I see a high percentage of an able-bodied population on
entitlement programs and collecting money for not working, I
wonder what is happening to this world. Back on the farm, if you
didn't work, you didn't eat. Work was honorable, and there was
little respect for those who appeared to be too lazy to work.

I am sorry for panhandlers I see on the street corners, begging
for money, when most of them could find some kind of work if
they wanted to. Perhaps their new-fashioned values won't let them
see *work* as a four-letter word of blessing, an opportunity to achieve
some positive level of self-worth.

Suppose half the population gets the idea that they do not have to work, because the other half is going to take care of them. And then the other half gets the idea that there's no use working when so much of their income goes to those who don't want to work. Can you see how this might be a problem? Maybe it already is.

Teenagers used to come begging to mow the lawn, work as maids, or babysit. A job flipping hamburgers or bussing tables at a restaurant was seen as a great place to start full-time work. Some kind of apprentice work or a *gofer* errand-running job wasn't too hard to find. To get a better job, they *worked* their way through college, because most parents didn't have the money.

Easy

The popular jobs today seem to be the ones that don't require much work. I've met sales clerks who seemed offended when they had to talk to customers. Is that what we really want, *easy* work? If you ever get an easy job that pays great money, you might not keep it for long. Lots of people would be looking to replace you.

The truth is, *easy* isn't as good as it looks. Back in the old days, we knew that. I had to work and study very hard before life became much easier. I had to survive a lot of tragedies to experience the triumphs. That wasn't easy. If the victories had been easy, I don't think they would have been worth much.

The *easy* courses in school require little work to make good grades, but then not much is learned, either. The *easy* jobs leave few opportunities for advancement. Apparently, *easy* is a good word only after it comes as a reward for doing a lot of work to get there.

Hard

I sometimes hear people say, "That's too hard. I'd rather do something else." Why do people say that? Sometimes it's the fear that they might fail, so they'd rather not try. So they guarantee their failure by not even trying.

Anything is hard when you don't know how. Learning can be hard when you know nothing about what is being taught. Perhaps the hardest part of life is refusing to give up when everything says you should. Why not give up? Because that's too easy, and there's no reward.

More and more, hard work seems to be something other people should do. I have spent a lifetime working harder than the next guy. Hard work caused me to get ahead in my career, but the journey would have been much tougher if I had thought "hard" was a bad thing. By embracing the "hard," I got to enjoy the "good" in my financial wellbeing and my sense of accomplishment.

I see fewer and fewer people putting in extra time and effort. Sometimes they want to do just enough to keep from getting fired. But if they wanted to help themselves, they would enjoy "hard" and do more than was expected.

Risk

By doing more than what is required, we risk having nobody notice. We might not get that promotion. We could still get laid off. That person who is so important to us might walk on by, paying no attention. Is it worth the risk?

I have a plaque hanging on my wall to remind me of a simple risk-taking truth: *If you skate on thin ice . . . you might as well dance.*

To make a friend, I must risk offending someone. Forget being politically correct. I'll be kind and considerate, but I must be myself. As hard as that is, I surely can't succeed at being someone else. I'll have to risk being me.

Along the way I have taken many risks, changing jobs, switching careers, and getting married. I carefully laid out plans that didn't work. I didn't always make the right business decisions. If I had avoided all risks, I would have missed all the things that worked. So risk is only bad when we do it without good purpose.

Save

Saving is something I started at age ten. I wonder how many youngsters follow that practice today. In the old days, we recognized the need to save for education and things we couldn't yet afford. We only bought what we had money to pay for.

Those values have changed. For many people today, the money they have is money to be spent, and if they don't have the money, then they use their credit cards until they are maxed out.

Over the years, saving was difficult. My wife and I had to do without what we wanted and cut back on what we needed. Saving required patience and sacrifice. Instead of "buy now, pay later," we used the old-fashioned values of "save now, have later." The result has been good. Very good.

Plan

In business, you may have heard about the importance of "planning your work and working your plan." But I don't see much of that in family life these days. Do high school students still learn how to open a bank account, control their spending, and balance their checkbooks? I doubt they learn about dating and marriage and that two people don't live more cheaply than one.

Most workers look forward to time off, but they haven't planned and saved money for an enjoyable vacation. More likely, if they take a vacation at all, they'll use credit to have fun and then add to their worries over how they will pay their bills.

A sound financial plan is important for both families and businesses. It may not be raining today, but we should have no doubt that a rainy day will come.

We're foolish not to have a plan. Make it a good one.

Hope

Hope was once something to fall back on when times were tough and life was uncertain. Our hope in God guaranteed life without pain and suffering in the age to come. But he also gave us hope in everyday life. As the apostle Paul encourages us with these words: "Whether well fed or hungry, whether living in plenty or in want, I can do all this through him who gives me strength" (Philippians 4:12–13).

My wife and I have faced every difficulty imaginable. Time and again, our trust in God carried us through. He gave us hope when there was no other reason to hope.

Without God, people have the government to rely upon for security. If they place hope in themselves, they will soon discover their weaknesses and realize how little hope they have. In the *Star Wars* movies, the Jedi knights were people's hope because they had the Force.

I find it strange that we can believe in the Force, but so many cannot put their trust in God, the true Force of the universe. No government or Jedi knight can secure our future like God can.

Today, God and church have become more of a convenience than a commitment. There is more reliance on self or government for hope, not so much on God. Living by what we used to call "a hope and a prayer" has turned to concern for our government benefits.

Pray

If "pray" isn't a bad word in modern society, I have to wonder why it's banned in so many public events. I'm not sure that "a time of silence" does much for a nation that needs God. A minute of meditation won't end the violence in our streets.

I think God is very disappointed when people don't want to talk to him. But I will leave that up to God to judge. I count this as one of the most important values.

Love

When I was young, love was a commitment for giving, for some degree of self-sacrifice. In marriage, it was for life, no matter the cost, in sickness and in health. We trusted the biblical values outlined by the apostle Paul: "Love is patient, love is kind. It does not envy, it does not boast, it is not proud. It does not dishonor others, it is not self-seeking, it is not easily angered, it keeps no record of wrongs. Love does not delight in evil but rejoices with the truth. It always protects, always trusts, always hopes, always perseveres" (1 Corinthians 13:4–7).

Today, love seems to be centered on a romantic feeling that ignores faith, trust, and commitment. It's more about what we can get than what we can give.

In my old-fashioned way of thinking, the world would be better with the old kind of love.

Grit

When slapped on the cheek, Jesus said to turn the other cheek and let yourself be slapped again (Matthew 5:39). Now that takes grit, which is more guts than it takes to strike back. We might think he didn't mean that, but the way he lived proves he did.

Today, a slap on the cheek is cause for a lawsuit to collect damages. The forgiveness preached in church is largely unknown in our society. We have the right to life, liberty, and the pursuit of happiness. So we hear a lot of whining from a world of unhappy people.

What happened to the old saying, "Grin and bear it"? Road rage is common, because so many people don't have the grit to forgive another driver's mistake. When life gets tough, they whine and complain and demand their rights. And that's from people who haven't seen anything as tough as what my wife and I have been through.

When times are tough, I often think of a statement made popular by American televangelist Robert Schuller: "Tough times never last. Tough people do!"

Without grit, we'll not overcome problems in life. I've not heard that word for many years, but people today could use a healthy dose of it.

Give

As our society has become more self-centered, the meaning of "give" has changed. Now, we seem to be taking as many selfies as we take of others. We're more inclined to grab than to give.

Four-letter words like wise, kind, and fair don't have the same meaning as they once had. People think we're wise when we agree with them. We're kind when we give them what they want. We're fair when we give them more than what we give anyone else.

The math for giving is difficult for some. Unless they recognize God as their resource for all they have, they think giving 10 percent of their income steals what they need for themselves. But if we're working to please the Lord, the math is different. The more we give, the more we get to give.

"Give," [Jesus said,] "and it will be given to you. A good measure, pressed down, shaken together and running over, will be poured into your lap. For with the measure you use, it will be measured to you" (Luke 6:38).

Nice

In all my years, I have never seen so much bitterness and hatred expressed by those who do not share the same political views. We seem to have forgotten the common old-time saying: "If you can't say something nice about someone, say nothing at all."

Sadly, we lie, cheat, and steal with our words. We claim honesty and transparency while being dishonest and secretive. We blame others for our wrongdoing and twist the truth to suit our own agendas. And that's not being nice.

If only we could follow the old-fashioned Golden Rule and always treat others like we want to be treated.

That would be nice.

Free

The "buy one, get one free" advertising ploy has been around a long time. Somehow, people began to believe business could give them something for nothing and not eventually go bankrupt. A store could double the price on a slow-moving item, then offer one for free, and suddenly the shelves were empty. How did we become so gullible?

It happened when we quit believing we should get an honest day's pay only after putting in an honest day's work. It happened when we quit believing we should pay a dollar for a dollar's worth of bread. It happened when we believed "free enterprise" meant we could get something for nothing. And now we're starting to believe the government can make everything free.

My grandfather used to say, "Somebody has to pay for anything that is free." We should keep that in mind because it's true, but we shouldn't stop there. If we're not paying, we should ask who is. Are we being charged extra for something else, so it only *looks* like something is free? If so, we've allowed ourselves to be duped.

Our government may be the greatest deceiver of all by leading us to believe it can give us benefits that we're not paying for. Most consumers cannot possibly find all the ways they're paying extra for a product off the shelf so we can have "benefits." On average, the sales price must include the seller's cost plus enough to cover all the business's income tax, Social Security, and Medicare tax withholding as well as all the taxes collected on the business itself. Anything less than that, and the firm must go out of business.

I'm not saying we shouldn't take advantage of free stuff. Jesus said, "Freely you have received; freely give." Just be aware that someone paid for your "free gift," and it's still not exactly free. Jesus said, "From those to whom much has been given, much will be required" (Luke 12:48 author paraphrase).

Politically Correct

In everything, do to others what you would
have them do to you, for this sums up the
Law and the Prophets. — *Matthew 7:12*

Perhaps being old-fashioned explains why I have so much difficulty with political correctness. If they teach this in school, I'd probably get a failing grade.

PC is a value that I have a hard time accepting—unless those letters stood for being properly considerate. That meaning I could handle.

A Bad Disease

The politics in political correctness is sickening. That's because I see only a superficial caring for others. The political correctness movement seems manipulated to suit people's personal goals. It's politically expedient to tear down statues and rewrite history as if the past didn't exist. Political opponents are destroyed by accusing them of something that was socially acceptable forty years ago.

I have trouble with the extent we have to bend our conversations and actions and can't be honest about our feelings for fear that someone somewhere might be offended. In the old days, "free speech" meant I could speak my mind without fear of being hanged. Not anymore.

Because I generally flunk this political correctness practice, my wife often tells me to keep my mouth shut when we are with people who have new-fashioned values.

I really don't want to offend people, but in today's world it seems that an awful lot of people want to take up arms against anyone who disagrees with them. In the old days, we call this "having a chip on your shoulder," suggesting that the person doesn't fit society's standards. Now, "being easily offended" seems to be a social requirement.

A lot of folks are making a very good living helping people to believe life is unfair and to see themselves as victims of anything they think is offensive. Anyone who chooses to speak freely, ignoring the Political Correctness Dictionary, is made an outcast, labeled as a mean and uncaring person.

Book Burning

In the days when I was little, my mother read to me wonderful books like *The Story of Little Black Sambo* and *The Tales of Uncle Remus*. Back then, children's hearts were warmed with such stories. No malice was ever intended, and people weren't offended. But now, you'll probably not find such books on any store shelf.

Some say Huckleberry Finn in Mark Twain's *The Tales of Tom Sawyer* was a racist. Mark Twain (Samuel Clemmons) would roll over in his grave, laughing, if he heard a news contributor say that. There was no such intention, but the political correctness police are too far removed from that era to understand history.

The classic movie *Gone with the Wind* has been attacked because it reveals a time when slavery was acceptable. Some are offended by the movie *To Kill a Mockingbird* because it doesn't fit today's political standards.

Instead of burning all the books and destroying all the movies that depict history as it really was, we should keep them and learn that there have always been bad and good people. By throwing away our history, I'm afraid we're encouraging more bad than good.

Tearing Down Monuments

Across the country today, we are tearing down monuments and destroying emblems because they are offensive to someone. The Jefferson monument has been challenged because the principal author of the Declaration of Independence and the third president of the United States owned slaves. At my university, poor old Jefferson's statue was smeared with paint because students didn't understand the statue's meaning from American history.

Apparently, they never learned that Jefferson established colleges like the University of Missouri, the first land grant university west of the Mississippi.

Here in Dallas, students voted to change the century-old names on schools because they were offended. Team mascots that were once positive icons for competitive intensity are being replaced for something that can't offend anyone. Why do we no longer call the Minnesota Vikings defensive line the Purple People Eaters? Are we offending people who might not want to be eaten? Let's change the rules so no one gets hurt, and call those huge defensive linemen the Pink Pansies.

The age of political correctness has made it next to impossible to erect any monument or choose a name that won't offend someone.

Colleges and Universities

Students have become so wrapped up in the spirit of "correctness" that they have become a mouthpiece for damning everyone who doesn't think like they do. While preaching inclusiveness, they have separate clubs, groups, and activities for the exclusion of others.

In the old days, our nation was known as a "melting pot" of different ethnic backgrounds, where everyone was viewed a "plain old American." Now we're more like a salad bowl, where every group wants to retain its own identity and judge which parts belong in their bowl. Some universities have "sanctuary places" where students can enjoy quiet and not be offended.

The education system's newfound political correctness comes at the expense of honesty, and in many cases, it's just plain silly.

Unsuitable Words

For a long time, "Islamic terrorists" could not be called out for who they were: terrorists. It was too much to call them radical. To be politically correct, what are we to call the people who want to kill us? With politically correct words, we're not kidding anyone but ourselves.

Society has changed so much that trying to compliment any ethnic group will either offend that group or another one. Any reference to Muslims, black people, or Indians can be dangerous. I just happen to be white, which I think should make me a "person of color." The Political Correctness Dictionary seems to change every day, so I find it difficult to come up with exactly the right words.

University Prejudices

When students at one university were offended by what others were saying, they organized marches, demonstrations, and boycotts. They claimed to be victims, demanded special treatment, and called for the university president to be fired. The media focused their cameras on people's anger and apparent injustices, promoting a wave of discontent that led to innocent people losing their jobs. Excellent leaders were replaced by others who could be more politically correct.

I scraped and saved and worked callouses on my hands just so I could go to that university. There wasn't time to even think about being offended. If students today had my old-fashioned values, they would be there to receive an education, not to voice their prejudices.

Christmas

After 200 years of celebrating the birth of Christ in this country, freedom of religion has become freedom *from* religion. I can hardly believe it, but nativity scenes now offend some people who consider themselves American. Religious Christmas songs are challenged and often banned in public schools.

In directing a wonderful forty-voice women's chorus during the Christmas season, my wife was asked to use "more secular" songs to avoid offending someone in the audience. Do you see what has happened to our old-fashioned values? The rise of political correctness caters to the few who might object while ignoring the less-vocal views of the majority.

In God We Trust

Our money says "In God We Trust" and our Pledge of Allegiance says we are one nation under God, but those are old-fashioned values. Public servants taking an oath of office used to finish with the words "so help me God," but that phrase is sometimes considered inappropriate and may be banned altogether. Political correctness stands against our heartfelt convictions and restricts our profession of faith.

How sad that we must now remove the Ten Commandments from our public buildings, because someone might read and follow them. Have we added to our suffering by eliminating the message, "Thou shalt not kill," from our schools? What have we done to the ethics of our military by forbidding chaplains to mention the name of Jesus? I wonder.

Newspeak

When I was in college, I read the book *1984* by George Orwell. I thought the idea that our government could control everyone's thinking was far-fetched fantasy, but not anymore. Now I'm seeing people unable or unwilling to think for themselves, eager to embrace whatever their political faction says is true.

In the old days, we took pride in the truth spoken by our news media and condemned the propaganda broadcasts by communist nations. But now I'm afraid we've become much like what we used to condemn. Too much of our news media is focused on appealing to a biased audience rather than properly researching and presenting objective truth. As in Orwell's book, newspeak seems to be the new language of the mainstream media.

Civility

In the age of political correctness, "civility" has acquired a new meaning. I'll skip the dictionary definition to tell you what it meant when I was young: "In your language and actions, be kind to others, even if they don't deserve it." But now, many would say it means, "In your language and actions, be kind to me, because I deserve it."

Many of those who tell me to be civil are the most uncivil people I have ever seen. The language of entertainers, athletes, and even the news media has reached a new height of vulgarity, nastiness, and just outright meanness. Cable television is filled with so much bad language, sex, and violence that I wonder if this society still has the right to call itself civilized.

The PC Bible

I have an opinion about what is going on. Political correctness makes big money for a lot of those who peddle it, very big money. Many proponents of the most radical parts of political correctness have made it a profession and have harvested millions by being consultants and speakers for their causes. Perhaps this is what we should expect from a society that ignores the Bible. Instead, we have the ever-changing, ever restrictive *politically correct bible* to guide people's speech and behavior.

Those who proclaim political correctness fail at their own advice. They are hypocrites. Jesus called the Pharisees hypocrites, saying, "Do not do what they do, for they do not practice what they preach" (Matthew 23:3).

Businesses know that "offended" people might march or demonstrate against them and might not buy their products if they are not politically correct in advertising. But the Holy Bible should be our guide, not the PC bible.

I believe in God, capitalism, and free enterprise. Ambition, accomplishment, and living within your means is important. Marriage and patriotism are essential parts of a God-fearing society. But behaviors and speech is more a matter of doing what is right, following biblical principles, than about being politically correct.

People with my old-fashioned values are often considered rubes, stupid, and unsophisticated—extremists who are out of touch with reality and still "cling to their Bibles and guns."

War against Biblical Values

So-called "progressives" have promoted a non-biblical lifestyle for decades and have won many battles. Our country is doomed if they win the war.

Many in Hollywood, the media, and technology are warring against all who do not support their values. What was abhorred fifty years ago has become acceptable if not desirable. The model family on television has changed from the housewife, working husband, and obedient children in *Father Knows Best*, *Leave It to Beaver*, and *My Three Sons* to dysfunctional families and shows like *Sex in the City*, *Desperate Housewives*, and *The Big Bang Theory*.

Be nice. Be civil. But, don't be foolish.

A lot of political correctness today is silly.

A lot is destructive.

My Fellow Americans . . .

Everyone who competes in the games goes into strict training.
They do it to get a crown that will not last, but we do it to get
a crown that will last forever. — 1 Corinthians 9:25

I rejoice in the progress we have experienced in America during my lifetime. My fellow Americans have built a great country. They have been amazingly generous to those less fortunate. They've fought and died to help people all over the world. There seems to be no limit to the good that my fellow Americans can do.

At the same time, I am saddened by all the good that has been lost.

Tarnished Greatness

Sometimes I wonder if our country is still headed toward greatness. In two world wars, over half a million soldiers died for our right to life, liberty, and the pursuit of happiness. We were the land of the free and the home of the brave, proud of our heritage and excited about our future.

Now, some say we should not regard our country as "exceptional." I question whether a past president could say, "America is not an exceptional country," if we had not lost ground. And when a presidential candidate can win with the message, "Make America Great Again," we can be sure many Americans believe we need to do something to remove the tarnish and restore our former glory.

Kill the Messenger

When a political or religious segment of society cannot defeat the message, the only way to destroy its popularity among the people is to kill the messenger. We've seen that practiced throughout history. Wanting to maintain control of the people, self-righteous Jews killed Jesus. His disciples would not have been martyred, had they not been a threat to political leaders. Radical Islamists seek to kill the infidels who disagree with them.

In the old days, we had a saying: "If you can't beat them, join them," which called for bipartisanship and negotiation. But now people seem to follow different values that say, "If you can't beat them, kill them," which says their way is right, and there's no room for negotiation.

What's wrong with wanting America to be great again? Everybody should want that, shouldn't they? But they don't. Why? Because it's a message from someone who isn't on their team, promoting their agenda. Since the message can't be argued against, they must do everything possible, even encouraging violence in the streets, to bring down the messengers.

Demonize the Righteous

What could religious leaders do when Jesus was saying so many wonderful things? He was healing the sick and delivering the oppressed. If they said he was a good, God-sent person, they would have had to join him, which they couldn't do. So they had to ignore the obvious and say he was doing the work of the devil (Matthew 9:34).

Seventy years ago, people were not so easily deceived. We recognized accusers who were guilty of the charges they were making against others, which we said was "the pot calling the kettle black." We don't hear that phrase today, probably because it would be judged racist. Back then, the expression had no reference to the color of a person's skin. But today we would make that association to avoid the truth that the accusers don't make themselves righteous by demonizing others.

58

What Your Country Can Do

In his inaugural address, President John F. Kennedy said we shouldn't be asking what our country can do for us, but that we should ask what we can do for our country. Today, I'm afraid that message would not be well-received.

Almost every day, it seems, some special-interest group is marching on Washington DC or protesting somewhere about what they see as the unfairness, mistreatment, and injustices of our country. They're demanding the very thing President Kennedy said we shouldn't ask, for the country to give us more.

The poor resent the more fortunate, who in turn resent the well-to-do, who then resent the rich, who will resent the super-rich. Everyone can complain about what they don't have, and we seem to be very good with campaigns for the government to give us equality.

Instead of working for their own success, people apply for food stamps and seek government assistance. They want compensation if an ancestor who lived 150 years ago was mistreated. They scream that this lousy country owes them more.

Years ago in my hometown in Missouri, anyone who complained what a lousy country we lived in would have been run out of town before dusk. We were very thankful to live in America. At my church, "Thank God for our country" was part of the elders' prayers every Sunday.

So, my fellow Americans, what can our country do for us? Not much unless its people quit complaining and do all they can for their country.

Illiterate America

In the early days after our country was established, most people couldn't read or write. That was okay, because we were a people who were working hard and striving to get better. Our one-room public school houses often used biblical text as reading material. We were on our way up.

Now, everybody can learn to read and write. The Internet provides a resource for just about everything we need to know. Yet literacy among much of our population appears to be on the way down.

I've read that a huge percentage of young men can't pass the basic test to join the army. If that's the case, they're not in a very good position to get a good job and support a family. Millions of illegal immigrants are flooding our country for the benefits of what is still the best economy in the world. But if they don't learn our language and understand our culture, they may turn to dealing drugs, theft, and other crimes instead of finding gainful employment. Some want to follow their own laws. How far might we be from violence in the streets like we see in other countries?

What a shame that so many coming to our country want the country they left, just with added American benefits. This clearly is a matter of values. I recall a statement by President Theodore Roosevelt that said immigrants must become a part of our culture in every way. We will not adapt to theirs. We have only one American flag.

I fear that we might see the day when educated people who can think for themselves and care about knowing and doing what is right could be a minority group.

Not What We Used to Be

We seem to be growing fatter but not smarter. Apart from the fitness fanatics, most of us are either obese or moving in that direction. No longer are we out on the farm, slaving in the fields all day. If we're not sitting behind a desk, we're on the production line where machines do much of the grunt work. We're burning less calories, but we still love a hearty meal at the end of a stressful day.

Our manner of dress has changed from coats, ties, and dresses to jeans, tank tops, and athletic shoes. But to really be in style, we need outer garments that look like underwear—or ripped and torn jeans that used to belong in the trash. Tattoos that were once reserved for crusty old sailors are now status symbols.

Loyalty to God and country is not what it used to be. Celebrities who make presentations at nationally televised awards shows have little to say about God, and they are often bad-mouthing America, the police, and others in authority. I'm sure such attitudes existed fifty years ago, but it wasn't as widespread and public as it is today.

What once was considered evil is now promoted as good. I'm not sure why networks still bleep filthy language, because we see it everywhere, on cable channels, at work, and on the streets. Lewd pictures and sexual acts condemned by the Bible and abhorred fifty years ago are now commonplace.

Common courtesies like opening a door for someone are no longer expected. They might even be taken as offensive. The use of words like "please" and "thank you" seem to be rapidly fading. A respectful response to elders with "yes sir" or "yes ma'am" was once popular across the South, but I don't hear it much today. People think nothing of answering their cell phones during a meeting. Even table manners have changed. Apparently, there no longer are rules for how to hold a fork or spoon or how to cut steak with a knife.

Business owners, bosses, and supervisors have lost the respect they once had. I see more of my fellow Americans complaining about how cruel their superiors are, making them work hard and not letting them have more holidays. I wish we respected our leaders and placed more value on our opportunity to work and make a living in this country. I wonder how far people are from thinking they shouldn't have to work. The government should support them.

My fellow Americans are deeper in debt, spending more and saving less. With each paycheck, they spend all they have and have little, if any, money to cover unexpected emergencies. The rate of bankruptcies and foreclosures has never been higher. Their need to work more or spend less is never considered, because they see themselves as victims of capitalist greed and the government not helping them enough.

What is most alarming to me is our blindness to the truth. People don't see anything wrong with their new-fashioned values. They accept the claims of their favorite entertainers and politicians without questioning whether they have been lied to.

Common Sense

Having had to make sacrifices all of my life in order to live within my means, I have trouble understanding excuses based on what people call common sense. From where I sit, "common sense" looks more like "insanity," but maybe that's just my silly old sense of values.

Our government somehow keeps extending its line of credit, so it doesn't have to worry about balancing the checkbook and being sure there's still money in the bank. After more than 200 years, our national debt passed one trillion dollars for the first time in 1981. Thirty-five years later, we were almost to twenty trillion. And that doesn't include liabilities for entitlement programs like Social Security and Medicare. We now seem to think adding a trillion each year is no big deal. Where will it end?

What kind of example does our government living beyond its means set for its citizens? Not a good one, I think. With the national debt so far out of control, I wonder when we'll declare bankruptcy. What happens to the value of money then?

Whose fault is this? Is it the politicians who make promises they can't keep, or is it the people who want to believe they can get something for nothing? Many of my fellow Americans are voting for more . . . because they claim to be "entitled." Others claim to be "offended" and want to be compensated for what they label as abuses to their ancestors. Again, they are looking for getting something for nothing without realizing that in the long run, we pay a high price in hidden taxes before we can get government benefits.

I see my fellow Americans demanding more controls and regulations by our governments at all levels. With every new tax, license, or government requirement, free enterprise is stifled and we pay more for goods and services. My old-fashioned values say we should scream, "Stop. Enough already." But instead, so many voters are begging for more "free" stuff.

Some have said, "Nobody ever went broke underestimating the intelligence of the American people." I wonder about that. I really think it's not intelligence but our new "common sense" values that are causing the insane changes we are seeing.

Faring Poorly with Welfare

Fifty years ago, welfare programs for business were virtually unknown. If businesses couldn't adequately match income with expenses, they failed, replaced by businesses with better

62

management. Now, too-big-to-fail bailouts and interest rate manipulation have become acceptable if not expected. What I find really offensive is when my fellow Americans rejoice because their stock market shares and 401K funds are supported in such a superficial way.

There was a time when both business and people did well without much government involvement. Perhaps we'd have more people and businesses wanting to work harder and do better if welfare and bail-outs weren't so easy.

Willingness to Work

Talk of everyone being paid, even if they don't want to work, makes no sense to me. But then, we already know how old-fashioned I am. If I didn't work, I didn't expect to be paid. And if I wanted to be paid more, I needed education, training, and skills that would make me worth more. My value depended on what I accomplished, not the number of hours spent "on the clock."

I believe *most* of my fellow Americans still have the ambition, determination, and values to block the socialist movement and get to work.

God Bless America

One pianist at my wife's choral group, The Mary Notes, grew up in Russia. "Too many Americans are spoiled," she said. "I am so fortunate to be here."

Bruni, a Mary Note, who grew up in communist East Berlin. She was separated from her parents and was sent to a camp for "readjustment" for her views. She celebrates every day that she lives in our country.

Diane is from South Korea. Her parents escaped from North Korea years ago. She has a wonderful attitude about our country.

Seven different nationalities are represented in The Mary Notes. They all thank God for America and get emotional when they sing, "God bless America." Just maybe, fellow Americans, we can learn from them about how great our country is.

At a Fourth of July concert, veterans like me were asked to stand. I was amazed. Nearly everybody was standing, men and women, most of them older folks who would again fight and die for their country. We cheered the flag and acted downright old-fashioned in our enthusiasm.

As I looked around with tears in my eyes, I beheld my *real* fellow Americans.

Hope for the Future

Wonderful changes are being made every day in our country. Contrary to what you might see on the news, it's not all bad. I could fill a book about the progress we are making. We are a creative, inventive people, advancing in science, business, and living standards. New ideas are springing up everywhere.

Life-changing and life-saving improvements are being developed at the fastest pace the world has ever known. I still see risk-takers. Courageous entrepreneurs are building new businesses with great new products.

Most important of all, I still see a high percentage of my fellow Americans practicing Christian values of love and generosity. Excited young people are pursuing their dreams and seeing their goals fulfilled. They may be a silent majority, but I still see most of my fellow Americans cheering the old-fashioned values that made our country great.

Millions of my fellow Americans work every day to make something great—for themselves, their families, and their country.

Drain the Swamp

Some people are content with the swamp, but many are saying, "Enough is enough. It's time to clean up the political mess." We need to quit talking political correctness and simply do what is right, returning to some of our old-fashioned values.

We're learning that we can't always trust the news media, the Internet, or the politicians who offer something for nothing.

The Right Education

I attend board meetings at my college of business, which has changed dramatically. Every year, over two hundred successful business people speak to students, preaching the benefits of capitalism, why it's still the most reliable path to success in history. Some of our students travel to Omaha to hear Warren Buffet, who says this group has an exceptional understanding of business and how to become successful. Another group visits Wall Street to talk with the world's most successful executives. Large groups study abroad.

For four years, how to achieve success is drummed into these young people. Most are employed when they graduate. There is a spirit there that makes me proud of what can happen in the right atmosphere. With a tear in my eye, I think it is indeed . . . a matter of values.

Old Values in a New Age

It seems to me that we must stand tall with many of the old-fashioned values that my fellow Americans still love—and would fight for. We can't let those who want full-time dependence on the government, with false promises of full-time pleasure, make good hardworking and patriotic old-fashioned folks appear to be a minority.

America can become greater. We have better technology. We have better resources than way back when. And we still have an overwhelming spirit and pride to achieve more and more.

We just need to put our old-fashioned values to work in this new age. We can't let politicians, Hollywood, and the media cast us aside. Never. Those old-fashioned values are what made our country great, so what our country needs is leadership that preaches those God-given values. We need to amplify, not diminish, our faith—like Roaring Lambs.

The Age of "Delightment"

Fools find no pleasure in understanding but delight in airing their own opinions. — Proverbs 18:2

Somehow in our pursuit of pleasure, we've lost the ability to have fun. In our desire for scholastic excellence, we're learning to score better on academic tests, even if we have to cheat, instead of learning to think for ourselves and discover truth. We seem to be more concerned with appearances than being open and honest.

Dumb and Dumber

Maybe it's my old-fashioned perspective, but I shudder over some of what I see happening in our country. It just doesn't always make sense. Many people's main goal seems to be entertainment. If it feels good, it must be okay. We want more. We want it all the time.

I like entertainment a lot, but I am not overwhelmed by it. I'm certainly not addicted, because other things are just as important.

Over the years, I have seen tremendous improvements in communication, which is good. But when entertainment becomes the substitute and obsession for hundreds of millions of people at the expense of other values, I believe we're showing how dumb we've allowed ourselves to become.

First Things First

We were once a people who worked hard first and played hard second. Those values built our country and gave balance to our lives. Our accomplishments improved our feelings of self-worth. Most communication came directly through face-to-face or voice-to-voice contact, not through the complex social media manipulations of today.

When a family of four sits at a table in a restaurant, each one focused on their cell phone, checking their social connections, we've let personal pleasure become the top priority.

Relationships are bound to suffer.

The Trillion-Dollar Entertainment Industry

Professional athletes now earn tens of millions of dollars each year. Do we know where that money comes from? Out of the pockets of those who buy tickets to events and will spend weeknights and Saturdays watching one game after another.

When I read the morning paper, the biggest part is the sports section, with page after page of pictures and details about the winners and losers. What was the quarterback thinking when he threw that interception? Going into the fourth quarter, was his shrug a sign of indifference, confusion, or what? I personally could do without all that analysis, but evidently it's important to most people, or we wouldn't see it in print.

If "delightment" has become people's focus, I'm afraid our care for spending face-to-face time with the family, helping the kids with their homework, and saving for retirement have become less important.

The Arts & Leisure section, which is half the size of the Sports section, glorifies entertainers and slams social injustice. Favorite entertainment spots and some of the best restaurants are highlighted with appetizing pictures.

The Business section is just a few pages, perhaps written mainly for old-fashioned people like me.

Television Everywhere

When I exercise each morning, I turn on the television and see the same kind of stuff: interviews of social celebrities and top athletes. Honestly, I'm not that impressed with the personal life of a young American Idol talent. It may be entertaining to most people, but my old-fashioned values take me to another channel.

On my computer, the host page is loaded with "news" stuff, mostly about entertainers, scandals, or something shocking. I could really waste a lot of time reading this mush, but why should I?

At the airport, I see people either watching television, talking on their cell phones, or texting. A few people seem to be working on their laptops, taking care of necessary business, but they are in the minority. Most find their "delightment" in whatever is showing on the television screen.

When my wife and I go out for breakfast, television screens are strategically placed for everyone's enjoyment. The music is so loud, I can hardly hear myself think, let alone carry on a meaningful conversation without shouting. This breakfast time seems to be more about scrambled minds than scrambled eggs. With my old-fashioned values, I'm looking for a quiet, relaxing restaurant where we can visit.

Addicted to Social Media

Today, we can communicate through Facebook, Twitter, LinkedIn, or a dozen other social networks I may not know about. Face-to-face conversation seems to be a lost art. In person, people don't know what to say, but they can text an instant response in seconds. I don't mean to say this is all bad, just the part that damages relationships through lack of personal contact.

I wonder what kind of lives people can have when they spend so much time broadcasting trivial details. At the end of the day, what have they accomplished?

Anyone who doesn't have a Smart Phone is thought to be not so smart. I'm wondering if all its wonderful features are taking us away from what a phone was originally designed for—to have a live conversation when the distance made it impossible to talk face-to-face.

I don't know why millions of people want to follow Lady Gaga and Kim Kardashian. Maybe they think this kind of contact makes them part of what they would like to be a meaningful relationship. In a miniscule way, they get to share the person's celebrity. Personally, I don't give a tweet.

A Person of Interest

Ask people who the first three American presidents were, and they'll do well to name the first: George Washington. Next, they might guess Abraham Lincoln, because they know nothing about John Adams or Thomas Jefferson. But ask them to name their top three movie stars or sports figures. They'll get that one in seconds, which shows where our interests are today.

The mainstream media plays for the delight of their readers, viewers, and listeners. Real news or educational stuff doesn't get much coverage. Is this because history is boring, or is it because the media has no desire to do extra work to show why historical figures deserve to be celebrities? I wonder.

For politicians to be elected, they usually have to be entertainers of some sort. Their education, experience, and voting records don't matter much. They just need a smile that looks genuine, a tone that sounds intelligent, and a manner that makes them likeable. Somewhere along the line, the basis for our values was distorted from facts to feelings.

Education

When I look around and see youngsters spending nearly all their time playing with high-tech games, cell phones, and electronic tablets, I wonder what parents are teaching their children. But then I see parents spending so much of their time playing with high tech gadgets. Then I know the answer.

Many have complained that our public schools are lagging behind other industrialized nations. That doesn't surprise me, if we are raising a generation more interested in playing video games than learning anything. We're teaching in order to push test scores up, but I'm not sure we're doing enough for students to see the importance of learning. When I see the misspellings on the emails I receive, I have to wonder how close we're coming to illiteracy.

Reading books for entertainment is not what it once was. Libraries are not crowded. Major bookstores are having financial problems. Some say printed books will soon be pretty much a thing of the past. We'd rather watch a video, which is about as mentally engaging as sleep. Reading takes time and effort, but it helps us think, and we learn about our world. It should never become "a thing of the past."

Too Much Delightment

Entertainment is wonderful. I love it, but when it displaces education, experience, and achievement, it has become too much of a good thing.

Has being entertained become our most important value? If so, parents should be concerned. They should scrutinize what their children are actually learning, or we'll have more and more young adults who have strong feelings without much knowledge of the truth.

When I was in high school I was invited to an FFA Recognition convention for an award. William Danforth, the founder of Ralston Purina was the speaker. He had an old-fashioned philosophy about how to have a wonderful and successful life. He introduced me on stage and gave me a book titled *I Dare You*. "Balance your life," he said to me, "and you will find success." He challenged me to loan that book to ten people, and I did. If he were to see society now, he would say we're out of balance.

We seem to be heading to the Land of Duh, where our yellow brick road is lined with delight. No failures, just fun. In my old-fashioned opinion, the Land of Duh isn't a very good place.

A Sporting Nation

Everyone who competes in the games goes into strict training. They do it to get a crown that will not last, but we do it to get a crown that will last forever. — 1 Corinthians 9:25

Values have changed a lot since the days when I was captain of my high school football team and was offered a small-college football scholarship. They have changed a lot even from when I was CEO of one of the top three sporting goods retailers in the country.

Toddlers Scoring Touchdowns

There was a day when toddlers learned to catch a ball *after* they learned to walk. But today, we're training our little athletes to be stars as soon as they learn to run.

Now, it seems like grade-school kids are being groomed for a career in the NFL. As soon as little Johnny learns to grip the ball when he runs off the right tackle, he's thinking past playing on the junior varsity team and seeing himself as leading his high school team in rushing.

I'm all for striving for excellence, but I'm afraid we've forgotten why we played the game. There was a time when it didn't matter whether we won or lost. It was all about how we played the game. We gave our best effort while respecting our opponents and treating them with kindness. Now, it's all about winning—at any cost.

Sparing No Expense

Our training programs have intensified at all levels. What was once taught in the professional ranks is now part of the university playbook. The high school curriculum has acquired college methods, with a large staff of coaches and assistants. The price tag is astronomical, but we're willing to pay it. We see the cost for better equipment, bigger stadiums, and the best coaches as a necessity. All this might be great if we weren't sacrificing academics to get there.

To play college sports, many of our high school athletes need private tutoring so they can barely slip past the minimum entrance requirement, which includes a need to read and write and do simple math.

Some people think college sports is a "cash cow," that universities receive billions of dollars in tickets and television revenue to support excellence in education. True, huge amounts of cash are received, but after scholarships, multi-million-dollar coaching salaries, travel and lodging, and other expenses, there isn't much for education.

The Wide World of Sports

Sports is big business. What used to be thousand-dollar salaries are now in the tens of millions.

At one time, parents could take their kids to a college or professional sports events without having to take a second mortgage on their home. The cost for attending the Super Bowl is far above most people's reach. Fortunately we can watch the game for free because companies are willing to pay millions of dollars for a few seconds of advertising.

In many states, the highest paid public employee is the university football coach. Who comes in second? That would be the basketball coach. Why is that? Because *The Wide World of Sports* is no longer a two-hour television show on Saturdays. It's a trillion-dollar industry fed by our insatiable appetite for entertainment.

Being Professional

There was a time when being professional included exemplary behavior and high moral standards. Pro athletes actually acted like someone children should look up to.

I'm thankful for all the athletes who still have great respect for God and our country. Under widespread scrutiny, they live with integrity. But I'm afraid these are not the people who get the media attention. Instead, the television camera wants to focus on those who kneel or raise their fists in protest.

Penalty Call

Rules were different when I was young. We didn't even have a full-time coach. We didn't have all the sports that are popular today. We had a football team, but we didn't have all the fancy equipment. Nobody was hired to stripe the football field. The players did that. Because we made sacrifices to even take the field, my getting to play for the state championship really meant something.

When our values are moving in the wrong direction, shouldn't an official throw his yellow penalty flag and mark off yardage? Apparently not. We seem more inclined to just change the rules.

There was a time when students were expected to graduate from college before entering the professional ranks. Education was important back then, but for many now, college is an opportunity for players to exhibit their physical abilities, and they will leave for the money as soon as they can. I admire those great college athletes who will say no to the pro draft and complete their education first.

The on- and off-field antics of so many just seems incredible. The full body tattoos, the horrible language, the unintelligent response to interviews, the strange clothes, the drugs, the drunkenness—all this is somehow popular. Officials won't throw a flag for anything not judged criminal. Instead, it's often glossed over by the coaches, the media, and crazed sports fans. No one seems to care that kids are looking at these people, thinking they should act like them.

Key to the City

One standout player in college football went to the pros for a multi-million-dollar salary plus millions in endorsements. But his illegal behavior landed him in prison. When he got out, he was back on the field, and the media gave him adoring admiration for "serving his time." In giving him the key to the city, the acting mayor said he was a "great inspiration" for young folks. Really? Surely we can find better inspiration for our kids.

A few years ago, one of the greatest boxers of all time passed away. Big articles on six pages in the Dallas Morning News raved about his greatness. His entire funeral received full television coverage. His amazing career deserved extensive coverage, but I had to wonder which parts might have led young minds astray. Was he a great hero for refusing the draft? I wonder.

Sports let me develop a spirit of competitiveness and confidence that has helped me throughout my life. I like to go to games and watch sports events on television. But when it becomes an addiction, I have to think our sense of value could be taking us in the wrong direction.

Plan B

Vision is wonderful, and you're not going to fulfill your dreams without focus on the goal. But what happens when things don't work out like we anticipated? We need a plan B.

I wonder about the kids who spend all of their time thinking, training, and believing their future is in professional sports. What percentage of these youngsters actually get there? Less than 7 percent will play at some college level, and less than 2 percent of those will make pro. Even if they do, their career is usually less than four years.

Excluding the elite few, 99.9 percent of graduating high school seniors need to prepare for life outside sports. With so much focus on sports and little attention to academics, I'm afraid too many are missing the all-important preparation for Plan B.

74

Getting Technical

*What do people get for all the toil
and anxious striving? . . . Even at night
their minds do not rest.* — *Ecclesiastes 2:22–23*

In simpler times we did not have all the high-tech gadgetry that we have today. We have made phenomenal progress in technology in the last twenty years, which is supposed to make life easier and better.

Wonderful Progress

Are we really better off now?

Most people can't remember what life was like fifty years ago. Only some 20 percent of the U.S. population is over age sixty. Graduating high school seniors don't remember the terrorist attacks in 2001. All they know of the Beatles, Rock & Roll music, and the assassination of President Kennedy are what little they've seen on the screen and in books. They've heard of typewriters but haven't seen one. They have no knowledge of life without cell phones and airport security screening.

If we're not careful, progress will be a problem because of the good we've left behind. I remember a quote from Albert Einstein, who was widely known and highly respected for his genius in the 1950s. I wonder how many young people today have even heard of him. He expressed fear that advancing technology would lead to a generation of idiots.

Our machines are getting so smart, we no longer need the mental and physical skills that were once essential for our survival. In our Information Age, we can be ignorant of history, because if we ever want to know, we can just Google it.

From Caution to Curiosity

I'm from the old generation that knew to be cautious. Check the temperature before jumping into the lake, and don't press a button until you know what will happen if you do. Smart phones and smart computers make me feel dumb, because I don't know what to do.

But my grandchildren know. They are part of the curiosity generation that sees a new button and says, "Oh, good! A new button! Let's push it and see what it does." Is that good? Yes, unless we've forgotten how to be cautious. In that case, if we're no longer in a fenced playground without those dangerous teeter-totters and merry-go-rounds, our lack of caution can get us killed.

Perhaps the younger generations would benefit from my old-fashioned values that say we should "look before we leap."

Time Savers

Before we had cars, horses pulling our covered wagons would get us from Dallas to Chicago in about two months. Now, it's an easy drive in two days or just two hours by plane. Before telephones, we had to go see someone to talk to them. Now we just grab our cell phone and can immediately see each other face-to-face, no matter where we are.

Advancements in technology have saved us an unbelievable amount of time, yet I hear more complaints than ever before about how little time we have. Why?

The number of minutes in a day is the same as it has always been, so what has changed? We now have more demand on our time, saying we should be making more money, accomplishing more, and having more fun. Our old-fashioned values that let us be content with what we had have been replaced with new-fashioned values of discontent. No matter how much we have, it's not enough. We want more.

Time Wasters

Money can be saved for a rainy day, but saved time has to immediately be spent wisely on something, or it's wasted. Back when we had to chop wood to keep the house warm in the winter, we got plenty of exercise and made good use of our time. But now that we have central heating and air, we must do something with the time saved. We might go to the gym for exercise, which may keep our bodies in shape but does little for our career unless we're an athlete. What do most people do with the four hours a day that technology has saved them? Watch television, play video games, or browse the Internet.

Wasting my time watching a TV show or movie that I've seen before makes no sense. I'm looking for something with a high return on the investment of my time. For sure, I don't want to share my every thought with hundreds of people on social media. I'm not sure why I should be interested in where people are and what they're doing all the time. I'm even less interested in cute pictures of their pets and the cake they baked.

It's been said that giving people a fish will feed them for a day. But teach a person to use the Internet, and they won't bother you for months, maybe years—unless you give them your email address.

The Latest and Greatest

Get a new cell phone, and it's soon obsolete. A ten-year-old computer is so old, it belongs in a museum. Whether it's cars, clothing, or the movies we watch, to be in style we need to own the latest and greatest.

A few years ago, I visited my cousin and her husband, Walter Schloss, who was considered by Warren Buffet to be the premier financial investor of all time. He never had a computer. He would not allow one in his home. "You can waste a lot of time if that is all you have to do," he said. "I have other things to do." He made phone calls by *dialing* numbers.

My wife and I own one car that is almost thirty years old. Our newest car is almost twenty. The old one costs less to repair than the newer one because a single part could be replaced rather than an entire assembly or system. We sometimes think of buying a new car, but I haven't wanted so much to be in style. I can be old-fashioned and save a lot of money.

Besides, in another ten years or so, both my cars and I will be antiques. By then, my cars will be more valuable than what I've spent, and just maybe my being old and wise will be back in style with its old-fashioned values.

Assessing the Value

When I see kids getting fatter and dumber spending hours and hours playing video games, I wonder whether this technology is a blessing or a curse. Old-fashioned parents used to cart their kids off to the library. If the distance from home to school was less than a mile, the kids often walked.

I wish more parents valued reading to their kids before bedtime more than watching their favorite television shows. In a restaurant, they should value visiting with the family more than what they're doing with their smart phones.

When a large percentage of a family's income is spent on the latest gee-whiz technology devices for Christmas, I am concerned. In a few years, most of "latest and greatest" will be obsolete, and they'll need to spend more. That might explain why I am content with my old-fashioned computer, car, and telephone, and also why I have more money for vacations, charities, and retirement.

Staying Poor

Everybody came into this world with nothing, but we don't have to stay that way. In the old days, "growing up" meant learning to live on our own, not living like babes dependent on others for their wellbeing.

I understand the need to help the poor and afflicted. Having a plastic card that looks like a credit card saves proud people the embarrassment of not being able to provide for themselves. But I can tell the difference between a credit card and a Lone Star Card. When I see people in the grocery checkout with their food stamps card, talking on their latest-model cell phone and then driving away in their late-model car, I'm thinking they've found a way to enjoy staying poor.

Years ago, nobody would think of doing that. But with today's values, it seems to be all too common.

Addicted to Video Games

I may be old, but I haven't lost my eyesight. I see what's going on around me. Sometimes I'm appalled.

Some really nasty video games are being played by teenagers and adults. Apparently, Pac-Man, Super Mario, and Donkey Kong games weren't good enough. Modern values say we need sex and violence, or we don't have a challenging, rewarding game.

If it were only a game, I wouldn't be concerned, but I'm afraid what we're addicted to on the screen promotes an appetite for the same things in real life.

In business, I discouraged employees from abusing their job by using their computer for playing games and doing personal business. Why was I looked upon as the bad guy? They couldn't be productive doing something other than their work.

Was the value of being entertained worth more than getting ahead in their careers? How could these addicts cheat their employer with stolen productivity?

They obviously didn't have my old-fashioned values.

Drugged by Technology

I've read studies that say an obsession with technology can change brain function just like a drug. As a player becomes lost in a game, dopamine levels change, regulating rewards, punishment, and euphoria the same as alcohol and drugs.

I don't think everybody becomes addicted. For some, technology is like fire, very useful when kept under control. But out of control, it can destroy a forest. Or a life.

Sue, Sweet Sue

The very fact that you have lawsuits among you means you
have been completely defeated already. Why not rather be
wronged? Why not rather be cheated? — 1 Corinthians 6:7

I remember days when lawsuits usually happened for good cause.
In the last fifty years, that seems to have changed. Dramatically.

Companies are sued. Government is sued. Individuals are sued
for just about any kind of cause, real or unreal. Even parents are
sued by their children.

We used to say, "Sticks and stone may break my bones, but
words will never hurt me." Not anymore. No longer are people free
to say what they think. They might be sued.

Liability for the Past

In the changing of our culture, what was once acceptable can be
politically incorrect today and the basis for a lawsuit. But it's not
just what we do and say today. It's also what we might have done in
the past. If that becomes known, even alluded to as a possibility,
people can be tried and convicted in the court of public opinion.

When a substance—asbestos, for example—is found to be
harmful, we would expect people to be liable for its promoted use
in products. But our modern values go further, not allowing
ignorance to be an excuse. Our past practices are judged by new
standards, because we could have known but didn't take the actions
that, in hindsight, could have been taken.

For the last two hundred years, we've not thought about suing
the government for mistreatment of our ancestors, but that
argument is viable today. What does that say about our changing

values? Lawsuits are often more about easy money, not so much about justice. Definitely not about forgiveness.

Finding Fault

Jokes have been told about no lawyers in Heaven. We know better than that. Many great people are lawyers, but if we saw the profession that way, the jokes wouldn't be funny. The common perception is that lawyers are there to steal, not give.

I am not against lawyers or the profession. Our daughter Mary was a trial lawyer and a very good one. Is it the lawyer's fault that society's values have changed, juries make judgments from different standards, and the legal profession has had to adjust to new demands? A little, perhaps.

But I'm thinking there's plenty of blame for everybody to share some responsibility for our changing values. What about our education system that has alienated God, or parents who could have taught better values to their children? The media has a special talent in making the important trivial and the trivial important. Some government leaders have been concerned for themselves and what their voters clamor for, playing partisan politics instead of doing what would be best for the country.

Liability Insurance

These days, we could be liable for anything, even hurting someone's feelings or hugging to recognize a person's value. Driving without liability insurance isn't smart at all. We need homeowner's insurance that protects us from a stranger walking across our yard and hurting his back. Doctors and other medical professionals must carry malpractice insurance to protect themselves from the *possibility* that with all their good intentions, something might go wrong.

I once received a letter that said I was entitled to receive payment because I had been victimized by a large retailer's advertising. I just needed to find the receipts and make my claim. In the very fine print, I read that the law firm was to receive 27 percent of the total settlement, which was $13.5 million plus $191 thousand in expenses and $2.45 million for mailings. Well, I was not offended enough to find four-year-old receipts so I could claim my $3. I just shook my head in amazement, wondering what our new values were costing us in liability insurance and higher costs.

The Ruling Class

We have a legal and political system that has allowed some lawyers to become incredibly rich and powerful. In a society that now wants to hold everyone accountable for everything, we pass laws for everyone except the lawmakers. What a brilliant legal maneuver, which should not surprise us, since most of the legislature are lawyers or people with a legal background. Lawyers making the laws. Could there possibly be a conflict of interest there?

At one time, the practice of law was considered a public-service profession in which it was illegal to advertise. Of course, the lawyers wanted to change that, because hundreds of millions of dollars could be made by encouraging people to file lawsuits.

As I was exercising while watching the television in the morning, three different lawyers were running their expensive ads, asking people with almost any kind of problem to call their 800 number. We used to call these people "ambulance chasers," but now it's regarded as just good business.

The Targets

Sue the police, the city, the county, or even an individual if that person offends your race, sex, ancestry, religion, or any other human right that the courts might respect. In general, any person or organization with money can be a target.

As CEO of several large companies, I became aware of many lawsuits filed for all manner of reasons, for almost anything you could imagine. Some were just plain frivolous. But the big suits were about the way a company handled its money.

Shareholder lawsuit lawyers run a multi-billion-dollar business, with settlements that often exceed $100 million.

Putting Sue to Work

Here is how the process works: The law firms find people who bought shares of stock and filed suit because they didn't get what they thought was a reasonable return on their investment. The lawyers then turn the suits into a class action so anyone who had bought stock during a certain time frame becomes a participant in the suit. Suddenly, the three or four individuals seeking payment of hundreds of dollars becomes a claim for hundreds of millions. The lawyers then name all the executives in another suit, making the original suit even more lucrative. They collect a third, plus expenses, which can wind up being most of the settlement.

Corporate officers spend countless hours providing information, testifying, and giving depositions. They worry that they might be facing personal damages and the loss of reputation. Before long, the company has invested a million dollars defending a lawsuit that was originally a small claim by a few people.

So what do company presidents typically do? They ask the insurance company to settle what might be a fraudulent claim rather than drag the mess on and on. The settlement will be much smaller than the claim, maybe a third or less. The lawyers get their millions for much less work, and the supposed victims get there few hundred dollars each.

Law firms that specialize in this practice usually succeed, but not always. Sometimes the company decides to fight, and they win in states where the company must be reimbursed for damages caused by the suit. Hardly any company will fight to the end. And these shyster lawyers know it.

War of Values

Medical and personal injury lawsuits were getting so out of control in the state of Texas that the legal system was changed. Awards were capped at a reasonable figure. What happened?

A miracle.

All of a sudden, the number of frivolous and fabricated lawsuits plummeted. Amazingly, the lawyer's values changed when there wasn't enough money to make their efforts worthwhile, which shows their true identity. They were always fighting to make money for themselves, not to help the "victim."

Creative Sue

When it comes to making money, lawyers aren't naturally good. They are trained to be good, always looking for the legal loopholes and weaknesses that will make them rich. Our elite law schools keep churning out ideas that are catastrophically bad for America.

From class-action lawsuits that promote the right to sue anyone over anything to court orders mandating the mass release of prison inmates—from the movement for slavery reparations to court takeovers of school funding—all these appalling ideas were hatched in legal academia.

The creative ideas confer power on legal intellectuals and their allies to supposedly litigate for people's rights when actually they become like kings who take advantage of the peasants.

Four Factors

I believe four factors contribute to an out-of-control legal system. They are all *value* things.

1. More of my fellow Americans now feel they are part of a "victim" class, because that status has been so effectively preached. Everyone is a victim of some injustice, and all can be compensated by filing suit for anything that offends. In our classrooms, students learn that capitalism is unfair, mistreating everyone except the capitalist tyrants who need to pay more to everyone, including those who don't want to work.

2. Juries comprised of my fellow Americans now feel that governments, corporations, and individuals are big and rich because they have taken too much from others and should be punished. They are often unaware of how little the plaintiffs will actually receive and how they are awarding tens of millions of easy money to the lawyers.

3. Politicians promote the atmosphere of being "entitled," not to benefit the people but so they can gain the control that makes the politicians rich.

4. People trust the hand they see feeding them. So they dislike lawyers and respect Congress even less. Yet they elect the person with self-serving interests, who most likely is a lawyer or has a legal background.

Not-So-Sweet Sue

My old-fashioned values tell me I shouldn't expect something for nothing. Any time people get a windfall, a lot of other people are paying for no benefit at all.

Who do you think pays when a big company is sued and pays millions in retribution and penalties? That money has to come from somewhere, maybe by reducing wages or increasing prices. Maybe the company goes bankrupt, passing that loss to other companies, investors, and individuals. Somewhere down the economic chain of events, the consumer inevitably pays for all the liability insurance, lawyers, and claims.

Our new-fashioned values encourage lawyers and clients to help themselves to easy money through frivolous lawsuits. And sadly, the news media and too many of the audience seem to rejoice and approve.

My value compass wonders how sweet this suing thing really is. I think I like my old-fashioned values better than what I'm seeing today.

Mind Your Manners

Do to others what you would have them do to you, for this
sums up the Law and the Prophets. — Matthew 7:12

My mother used to say, "Mind your manners, sonny." Those
repeated reminders told me manners were important. At least they
were back then. What about today?

Being Respectful

When I was little boy and said something that was rude or
disrespectful, I could get a swat on my bottom. In those days,
elders were to be respected, even if I thought they were wrong.

We now live in a fault-finding era of disrespect. The media helps
us with that by headlining misbehaviors as if everyone within a
classification is bad. If 99 percent of our police officers are kind,
just, and caring in the way they deal with people, including
criminals, but if the media shows only the one who misbehaved,
what is the audience led to believe? If we're not careful, that 1
percent can cause us to make incorrect assumptions about the 99
percent.

Wrong Assumptions

The way we perceive others has a huge effect on our relationship
with them, changing what we say and do. If we think a police
officer is out to get us, to make our life difficult, we are more likely
to react in a disrespectful manner that makes us look criminal, even
when we aren't.

My old-fashioned values led me to think others had good
intentions, even when their expressions and words were harsh. So

how did I react? With kindness and respect, and I almost always found them responding with a smile, eager to help me. With just a little respect, I made a friend instead of an enemy.

Today, I'm afraid our new-fashioned values expect bad intentions, even when people's expressions and words are kind. After we've already, in our minds, made others out to be enemies, we aren't likely to ever see them as friends.

Road Rage

Rudeness on the road is common, sometimes in disrespect, but at other times, just from not paying attention. Years ago, that wasn't a big deal. We could ignore such behavior and drive on. But now, we know to take offense at a perfect stranger who may not even know we exist. Sufficiently angered, we might react, trying to teach manners to the offender. That's not a good idea. I don't recommend it. Old-fashioned values are better. Drive on, and try not to let your blood boil.

One day, I was driving to the bank when a young woman pulled across two lanes of traffic to cut me off, then sped up the street. She pulled into the parking lot, just ahead of me. We were going into the same bank. I reached the front door before she did, and I opened the door for her. No smile, not even a thank you from her. She rushed to the counter, obviously wanting immediate service.

Apparently, that young woman didn't have an old-fashioned mother like mine. If my mother had seen me cutting someone off, pushing others away so I could be first, she probably would have given me a swat on the butt.

Respect for the Law

As I observe others going down the road, I see speed limit signs that are either to be ignored or taken as suggestions for how much faster they should go. No matter what the legal limit is, they think it's okay to go faster.

When driving down the freeway, I stay in the right lane to avoid speeders and try to save my life. In congested traffic, impatient drivers crowd dangerously close behind me, as if to push me forward. When traffic clears, they speed around and pull in front, as close to me as possible, just to show that I have somehow offended them by driving the speed limit.

Uncommon Courtesy

The apostle Paul writes about the importance of being kind to others, making their needs more important than our own (Romans 12:10). There was a time when that advice was valued, but today, behavior that was once considered "common courtesy" has become uncommon. After others are kind to us, only then will we consider being kind to them.

People seem to be so focused on themselves and their concerns, they can't even smile and courteously acknowledge a stranger walking by. We're too busy talking on our cell phones, texting, or checking our social network to be sociable in real life.

In a meeting, someone's cell phone rings. That should be embarrassing, but instead of silencing the ring, the person answers and begins a lengthy conversation. Before the movie, theaters remind the audience to turn off their cell phones. Great idea, but I have to wonder why I still hear phones ringing. Were people so focused on themselves that they didn't see the message? I wonder.

Children watch their parents and quickly learn that it's okay to disregard other people's feelings. At the grocery store, I was almost run over by someone talking on the phone while pushing a cart. Maybe the call was that important. I have no way to know. But when the person didn't even say, "Excuse me," I have to wonder about values. If I had done that as a youngster, my mother would have said, "Mind your manners, sonny."

Ruined Party

I love parties, but not at the cost of ruining someone else's party. I was once given the Golden Rule that I should treat others like I would like them to treat me. Those values aren't what they used to be.

My wife and I celebrated my birthday at a fancy high-priced restaurant downtown. I had anticipated a wonderful evening, but it didn't turn out that way. The people sitting at two large tables near us were on their cell phones, either showing pictures or taking pictures. As they kept drinking, they became even louder, making the rest of the room uncomfortable. They didn't seem to care. Apparently, they didn't know about common courtesy.

Bad Language

When we are so focused on ourselves, we can be oblivious to the fact that others are hearing what we say. Jesus said, "Out of the abundance of the heart, the mouth speaks" (Luke 6:45). But in this age of political correctness, I'm afraid we're letting our mouths run without our minds being fully in gear.

In ages past, if you hit your finger with a hammer, you were allowed to cuss. But that language was not something we heard in everyday conversation. That would have been "bad manners." When I was growing up in King City, Missouri, my teachers wouldn't tolerate any kind of foul language. People who cussed a lot were shunned as real lowlifes. Now, bad language is so popular among some groups, we seem to be competing for who can say the most foul words.

Fifty years ago, most of those expressions would never be heard in public. Some young people today feel they are more "hip" because they use terrible and embarrassing language in talking about anything. But what really bothers me is how profane some politicians in our country can be when they speak to their constituents. Yet the audience cheers. That doesn't speak well of their values, does it? When network coverage has to bleep out the words, what kind of an example does this set? If I had talked that way as a child, my mother would have washed out my mouth with soap.

Celebrity Insanity

The celebrity awards shows on television amaze me. They take the concept of short skirts and revealed cleavage to a whole new level of indecency. Presenters seem to be competing for who can use the most foul language. Fifty years ago, such behavior was unthinkable. If my mother could have seen it, she would have said, "Oh my God!" and fainted from shock. But today's audience cheers and asks for more.

Some of our biggest celebrities in athletics, entertainment, and social circles have perverted good manners to present nudity, drunkenness, and filthy language as something desirable. I don't blame these fools as much as I blame my fellow Americans for adoring them.

Pigs at the Table

When I'm eating at a restaurant, I can't help but notice the manners of others who are eating out. I see them dive into their meal without waiting for others to be served. With their elbows on the table, they shovel in the food. They talk with their mouths full, chewing at the same time. They grip their fork like a scoop and wield a knife as if the steak might crawl off their plate.

When I was on the farm, my pigs had better manners.

My old-fashioned values say we should be considerate of others at the table, know how to hold a knife and fork, and chew with our mouths closed. At a restaurant, we should frequently thank our server and not walk away without leaving a tip.

I've heard that Christians have a reputation for tipping little, if anything, which makes me sad. We should be a better example of kindness and generosity.

Running Wild

In public places, I often see children running wild. Even in churches during worship, we might see them wandering the aisles, standing on the pew, or crawling underneath. There was a time when we had no "children's church." Youngsters were taught to behave, and they learned quickly after a few trips outside for a spanking.

My son-in-law, who grew up in Germany, knew how to handle Jonah, our grandson, who would test the limits of manners in public places. "Jo-o-o-nah," he said, "we are about to go outside and have a man-to-man talk." Jonah knew this was not an idle threat but a promise for something more than talk, and that ended the bad behavior right then.

Today, parents using the "board of education" might be arrested for child abuse. I can only hope that children's church can teach them what they are often unable to learn from their parents.

Flying Our Colors

I don't think there is a better place to see really bad manners than on an airplane. I quickly see who are focused on themselves and care nothing for others. Instead of showing us how to fasten our seat belts, flight attendants should teach passengers something about in-flight courtesy.

As soon as the plane arrives at the gate and the bell sounds, everybody is up, crowding the aisle, and grabbing for their luggage. I'm thankful for those who will reach up to the overhead bin to grab a suitcase for someone else. Occasionally, I will see someone wait patiently while a mom struggles to get out with her children. I would love to see more of those old-fashioned values of honoring strangers by helping them.

Fool's Gold

Not everything that glitters is gold. But it looks like gold, and that's the problem with some of our new-fashioned values. We want to be treated well, to be loved and appreciated, so we are quick to notice the slightest offense. We see all the injustices in the world and join the protests, demanding change. Our fool's gold motto is, "Do as I would have you do unto me, for what you're doing now is not good enough."

The real gold requires some attitude adjustments. There was a time when we called it, "The Golden Rule." Instead of focusing on the behavior of others, which we can't change, the principle looks at how we can help ourselves by being kind to others, even when they don't deserve it. Jesus presented this old-fashioned value in his Sermon on the Mount, when he said, "In everything, do to others what you would have them do to you" (Matthew 7:12).

Jesus said this is the premise upon which all the biblical guidance from the Law and the Prophets was built. If we would follow The Golden Rule, our manners wouldn't be a problem.

Driving with Idiots

If it is possible, as far as it depends on you,
live at peace with everyone. — Romans 12:18

The Golden Rule should apply to every aspect of our lives, but the one place I see it least used is on the road.

Off to the Races

I see cars racing past at speeds far above the limit, weaving in and out of traffic, obviously in a hurry. Sometimes they are just one slight misjudgment away from a tragic accident. I wonder how much stress they must be putting themselves through, and for what? I often catch up to them at the next traffic light.

Maybe I'm the idiot for being careful and obeying the speed limits, but I don't think so. With safer driving, fewer traffic tickets, and less stress, I may live longer.

Road Rage

At times, I'm almost afraid to drive. What I see on the road can be a cause for frequent prayers. I confess, the muttering of my thoughts, calling people idiots, isn't the best thing to say aloud.

When riding with me, my wife said, "Don't let them hear you. They might shoot you." That was my signal to let cooler thoughts prevail.

Webster says an idiot is a foolish or stupid person—in other words, someone whose thinking isn't right. Or maybe it's not thinking at all. Too many times, drivers react in anger, without thinking. They might pull out a gun and shoot someone, then spend time in prison for their thoughtlessness. Now that's idiotic.

Out of My Way

Unsafe drivers, who speed through congested traffic and ignore the laws, aren't trying to be idiots. I think it is more of a value thing.

My old-fashioned values just don't match the new-fashioned values of many drivers. Because they are in such a hurry, I am obviously in their way. Patience is not as important to them as it is to me.

I drive more carefully than many people, and I try to be considerate of other drivers. I don't text or talk on the phone while driving. You won't see me with one hand on the steering wheel, the other holding a hamburger. I won't be speeding through the parking lot to reach an open space before anyone else. My old-fashioned values will let them have the better spot, and I'll get much-needed exercise by parking farther away.

One-Fingered Salute

As cars whiz past, I am pressed to drive faster. I don't like being flipped off by passing drivers, but I get the message. They want me to break the law like so many others. Occasionally, they give me a one-finger salute. Sometimes they honk. Their values about speed limits are just, I guess, different from mine.

Tailgating is against the law in Texas. So is excessive speeding and texting while driving. Don't they teach that in Driver's Ed? Of course they do, but our new-fashioned values seem to say it's okay for them to make their own rules. And give a nasty salute to those who don't drive like they do.

The Worst Offenders

I'm guessing that most offenders never went to Sunday school—at least not like the one I attended in King City, Missouri. I don't think their goal is to offend. They aren't idiots, not really. It just seems that way because they show so little regard for others.

Because they never learned the importance of The Golden Rule, they are thinking only of themselves. They are just very self-centered.

The roads would be a lot safer if they could learn some old-fashioned values.

Color Outside the Lines

Let us stop passing judgment on one another. Instead, make up your mind not to put any stumbling block or obstacle in the way of a brother or sister. — Romans 14:13

My definition of racism is prejudice against a class of people because of their ancestry and color. That's just not who I am. So I don't like being called racist. Not one bit.

Mislabeling

During the last few years, a popular means of attacking people for their beliefs is to declare them racist. In doing so, they separate themselves and promote the division and strife that they supposedly want to eliminate. Their actions don't match their words.

I'm all for labeling a problem when and where it exists. But that's not how the term is being used today. Instead of identifying a problem and promoting solutions, it is used to attack those who don't share the same ideologies.

The problem with mislabeling is how often people don't look behind the label to see if it's true. Dr. Martin Luther King championed a movement to recognize and resolve social prejudices. But modern celebrities heighten people's fears and resentments. They preach racism to bolster their own popularity, prosperity, and power.

When in office, President Obama missed a wonderful opportunity to reduce racial prejudice in this country. I can't judge his motives, but he seems to have made assumptions and applied racism labels where they didn't belong.

I believe our former president Jimmy Carter said most of my fellow Americans are racist. That may have been his opinion, but it needs further definition and research to make it a fact. When people read the label, they think "most" applies to everyone. They see the offense without recognizing how often it doesn't apply. For their political agendas, the feeling is what matters, not the facts.

Guilty by Accusation

I heard a presidential candidate in 2016 say we are all racists. Really? That's an accusation that makes everybody guilty without defense. When people hear a lie long enough, they tend to believe it's true. So their belief changes their actions, which makes it appear to be true—what we might call a "self-fulfilling prophecy."

Our new-fashioned values have popularized name-calling. To prove abuse, people will fabricate stories that stir people's anger. Later, after someone's video disproves the claim, the damage is already done, because so many are quick to believe the accusation.

After they've believed the accusation, they may not see the contrary evidence. Even if they do, they may choose not to believe, because it's very difficult for people to displace what they already believe is true.

I long for the old-fashioned days when our culture doubted accusations until after they were proven. But under today's values, that seems to be too much trouble. We'd rather judge by the accusation and not expend effort to know the facts.

Our laws say a person is innocent until proven guilty, but that's only true in our courts. In our society, people are now judged and sentenced according to what our respected leaders say about the accusation.

Persecution in Uniform

When a million people in this country work in law enforcement, we'd be insane to think every officer is perfect. Some have bad motives and break the laws they are sworn to uphold. It's equally insane to believe every police officer is out to get us, especially if we're not white. But that's where our modern values seem to be taking us.

I'm bothered by the chants I hear on the news. "Pigs in a blanket—fry them like bacon. What do we want? Dead cops. When do we want it? Now, now, now." I'm all for freedom of speech, but I'm not for the media promoting this language as something we should do.

Promoting Inequality

I read a newspaper editorial that said racism is not over. Of course. We live in a sinful world, so what makes that "news"? If it were over, we'd have no reason to write about it. People might live in peace with their old-fashioned values, in honor preferring one another. But to sell newspapers and have good TV ratings, we need to keep our perception of inequality going by saying it's not over.

The term "white privilege" is used to promote the feeling of inequality so the voting public will unseat those in authority, people who have built highly successful businesses. Supposedly, the reason we can't be successful is because of all those "white privileged" people. But without them, most of us would lose our jobs. Somehow, we've overlooked that fact.

What really bothers me is how people of color are demonized when they become highly successful. People who really want the best for the black community are labeled as "Uncle Toms," as if they too are part of the "white privileged" community.

A lot of people are enjoying luxury living by promoting inequality. While professing "inclusion," they promote the opposite. They continue to encourage exclusion, not inclusion, widening the separation between groups.

Colorless Community

Growing up in my small rural town in Missouri, I paid no attention to the color of people's skin. Color only matters when we're taught that it matters. When I was a boy, I got to know two black men who were business associates of my father and grandfather in their mule trading business. Their color didn't matter, because they were great family friends.

I think it's the character of the person, not the color, that should matter. I strongly supported inclusion of all ethnic groups. I depledged the fraternity that flew the Confederate flag. I thought that was just plain silly. And I strongly hated the injustice of inequality that I saw back then. Decades later, we should be doing much better, but that doesn't seem to be the case.

Maybe we need some of my old-fashioned values that say color doesn't matter. But as long as we're paying attention to color, I'm not sure we can do that.

The Color of Laziness

In my past business experiences, I supported everyone who wanted to work hard and get ahead. No matter their color, if they showed superior performance, I wanted them on my team. Period. Black, yellow, or brown people got ahead at the same rate as others. But color them lazy, and I had to discriminate—and that's legal, a necessary part of building a successful business.

I understand that black people might have cultural obstacles to overcome. But so do some white people. We all do, to varying degrees. When I saw the extra effort of those who had much to overcome, I encouraged and rejoiced in their successes even more.

America's Flying Colors

We are a mixed breed that spans more than two centuries. I'm sorry for people who make skin color an issue, because those lines have blurred since the founding of our country. We should all fight discrimination because of color or creed.

As president of her college sorority, my daughter took on the national leadership because others were discriminating. That created quite a stir on her campus, perhaps causing her to lose the election to be student body president. Her actions were not popular. Her old-fashioned values said she had to do what was right, and I was proud.

My daughter who lives in Charleston, South Carolina, is a member of a gospel group that is 90 percent black. Many of her closest friends are black, yellow, and brown.

My granddaughter was a finalist in a statewide contest with a paper titled "Unity." Like so many others in my family, her favorite color is American.

Misrepresentation

When things are not equal, we deceive ourselves when we say they are. Some news agencies would have us believe that police forces across the country are racist, because more minorities are arrested than whites. That's a distortion of the numbers, given the fact that crime is seven times more likely in black communities. The problem is criminal behavior, not race.

By distorting and misrepresenting the numbers, the pot is constantly being stirred to a boiling point. I see more hatred coming from the minority population today than any time of my life.

Trillions of our tax dollars have been spent on welfare, food stamps, and affordable housing. Governments, businesses, and colleges have discriminated in favor of minorities. That effort hasn't produced the positive results we intended, perhaps because we're treating symptoms instead of the problem.

Immigrants have been invading America from the time it was first recognized as a land of opportunity. I do not blame people for wanting to enter our country and harvest a wealth of benefits. I would do the same thing. No prejudice on my part. But I don't like politicians ignoring the facts, using this issue as a basis for their own gain.

Some people are offended when anyone says Islamic terrorists might be killing innocent people in the name of Jihad. I am offended when Islamic extremists kill Christians and anyone they disagree with, including other Muslims.

My value system says discrimination is a terrible thing for our country, and those who focus on the problem for personal gain, instead of adding to the solution, make matters even worse.

The Right to Riot

You have spent enough time in the past doing what pagans choose to do . . . They are surprised that you do not join them in their reckless, wild living. — 1 Peter 4:3–4

In recent years, the perception of rioting has changed from a criminal attack on our nation to a justifiable expression of free speech. My, how our values have changed.

Political Justification

Who gives people the right to violence and the destruction of property? Our laws may be against it, but they have to be enforced. Some are prosecuted, but others are released with little more than a warning. Many others are never arrested.

In the court of public opinion represented in our news broadcasts, rioting seems to be something we should expect when an injustice has occurred. Since an accusation is all that society needs to perceive guilt, we have people rioting over imagined offenses, something that didn't actually happen.

If politicians and newscasters who condone rioting had their own property destroyed, they might want to change their message. Those who have seen their homes and businesses burned and looted, their families, employees, and associates endangered, have a different perspective on rioting. I know that from personal experience.

Police are shot and hospitalized or killed. Public and private properties are destroyed. Entire communities have been leveled and never replaced. Unlike "acts of God," we could change this if we wanted to, if we would preach doing right rather than telling people what helps their political agendas.

Close-up View

My values are a lot different from many well-meaning people, because I've experienced rioting close-up. Journalists and photographers keep their distance as observers, but the victims experience what is really going on.

Sympathizers may claim that rioters are just disadvantaged young people who grew up in bad conditions and have a right to express their anger and frustration in this way. The rioters are seen as victims, not victimizers, from unjustly crowded slums with insufficient government benefits. The police and the outside world treat them unfairly, so we can understand why they would riot, loot, and destroy property.

Closer inspection would reveal a problem where people see an opportunity for criminal behavior without a long prison sentence if they are arrested. Poverty isn't the problem.

In my little rural town, we lived far below the poverty line drawn by today's standard. There were no riots. No demonstrations. Sweetie Miller, the local sheriff, would have quickly locked up rioters in the local jailhouse. Our community would have been outraged if looting and destroying property had occurred, no matter who the violators were, whether black, white, or purple. They were criminals who belonged in jail.

We would do well to return to those old-fashioned values.

Lynch Mob

Angry people want to hang the person they think is guilty, without due process in which the evidence is carefully scrutinized. Take the Ferguson, Missouri, tragedy for example.

A white police officer shot an unarmed young man. That's all people needed to know. Some politicians and news media threw gasoline on the fire. Our president, attorney general, and the Missouri governor got into the act, condemning the officer. They agreed with what they perceived to be the rioters rallying cry. We must stop police brutality. That was a political ploy to gain votes rather than calm the people with reassurance that we must abide by our laws of due process, or we will hang the wrong people.

Further investigation revealed the truth. The officer had correctly responded to a man who had beaten him and was going for his gun. Eventually, a grand jury and the U.S. Justice Department refused to throw the rope around the officer's neck. He wasn't guilty, but the minimal media coverage of that fact did little to change the mob's opinion.

In Baltimore, Maryland, the city attorney said, "This is your moment." The lynch mob was to get what they wanted. Their protests were justified. Yet again, the race baiters were stirring the pot for sensational media coverage and political gain. When the six officers were acquitted, politicians called for more protests.

Rioters are victims of those who promote anarchy, allowing political rhetoric to shape their values. If only they had some of my old-fashioned values, they might not be so vulnerable.

Political Spin

I keep thinking our politicians are largely responsible, because they cater to the problem rather than pointing to the truth that would bring solutions.

Just maybe, if these young toughs had two parents and a job, they would have better self-esteem and want to contribute to a prosperous society rather than burn and loot it. We might appreciate what officers do for us, not want to kill them.

By taking prayer out of the schools and subjecting Christians to public ridicule, we distance ourselves from the fundamental biblical truths that could save our nation. Those old-fashioned values served us well for two centuries. Without them, I'm afraid we have become our own worst enemy.

Political spin continues to promote division that could be fatal. Jesus said, "Any kingdom divided against itself will be ruined, and a house divided against itself will fall" (Luke 11:17). I fear for our country if we cannot stop the political spin.

Deplorable People

On talk shows, those who love our country and appreciate our history have been portrayed as ignorant and out of touch with reality. Since the commentator's view is assumed right, everybody else must be wrong, deplorable in the sense that we can't endorse their truth.

They may think I don't understand, but I do. I have been there. I have lived with the problem. I managed inner-city businesses during rioting and experienced property loss and the fear of what might happen to employees. I have seen the social and emotional devastation after a place of business is burned down, leaving people without jobs and little hope for recovery.

I grew up in a town where the law was to be obeyed, not argued against. People earned their success through hard work. We didn't want government support, let alone expect it. We went to church and believed the Bible. With those old-fashioned values, I am deplorable. I see no way that our new values will take us to the peace and prosperity that some politicians promise.

Not a Great Feeling

Soon after I was promoted to be JC Penney's sales and merchandise manager for about thirty stores in Milwaukee, the rioting started. Rioters burned and looted. They injured people. They did millions of dollars damage to homes and businesses owned by people of all colors.

I had to decide what to do for the safety of our associates who worked in those urban areas. Many stores were already under siege. I had a serious problem on my hands. We closed all the stores and evacuated the associates. As I walked their path, I knew my life was in danger. That was not a great feeling.

What came next was worse. Over 200 days of marches promoted "black power." Some members of the Black Panther organization robbed those who exited a white-owned business. You can imagine what this did for daily sales. The police saw themselves as powerless, because they did not want to set off more riots.

Good hard-working black families became the prey of local terrorists. Their businesses burned, turning hope into hopelessness. "Opportunists" took advantage of the situation. They threatened further devastation if the owners refused to pay for their protection. My company was one of the worst hit by this scheme, because we were large and visible.

102

All this happened during the administration of President Lyndon Johnson, who established the largest system of welfare in the history of our country, called The Great Society.

I wasn't feeling that great.

The Misconception

I was vice-president of a department store chain that successfully operated stores in difficult urban areas. Our store in Liberty City had the largest black population in Miami, Florida.

Supposedly, riots started because Hispanic police, who were later acquitted, tried to stop a crime and shot a black man. Rioters stole everything they could—millions of dollars of inventory. They were not thinking about their ancestors being slaves. Most of them were from Central and South America.

For fear of setting off another riot, the looters were never punished. Sixty employees were immediately left without jobs, and in the coming Christmas season, a hundred people would have to find work elsewhere. I was left to figure out what do with the remaining rubble and reclaim the battered safe.

A Difficult Decision

My company had to make a tough choice. Would we rebuild or give up on the community?

We decided to rebuild. We were the only department store in the area, built next to a new supermarket. We wanted to be a positive influence in the community. With a lot of hard work, we were pretty successful. However, it was not long before the new supermarket went out of business. The theft was just too high. "Community organizers" protested that the owners were "racist."

The next year, our intelligence picked up rumors that more riots were coming. We were warned by the good people in the community. They didn't want their only department store burned down again, so we were prepared.

The Army National Guard was activated and camped on our parking lot. We suffered no damage to the building or its contents. But we did lose a lot of business. The rest of the community was again burned, including the vacant supermarket near our store.

I would like to say this was the end of rioting in this community, but it wasn't. The next year brought more terrorism. Apparently, people had become fed up with modern politics and new-fashioned values.

The good law-abiding citizens gathered in our parking lot, joined hands around our building, and turned back the looters. That really happened. They didn't want the nicest store in the area to be looted by thugs. This gave me hope that our old-fashioned values might be restored.

Cause for Retreat

There came a time when the fight could no longer be justified. Most of the good people in the community moved away. We closed the store.

After we closed the store, the former district manager wanted to lease our old building and start a new department store. With mine and other references with lenders, he had the financial backing. But the community organizers wanted to "help him run the store." Lenders said he was crazy to locate a business where so-called leaders would have control. His business never happened. He too had to retreat, becoming successful elsewhere as senior vice-president of a large retail company.

Now, the area is a crime-ridden welfare plantation of dependency. Small stores are barely able to survive. I can only hope and pray that the community gains some old-fashioned values.

Unworkable Values

What happened in Liberty City still bothers me, because the values held by the hustlers and organizers assumes that the rich people are being unfair and the government isn't helping them enough. The population is agitated into believing that class warfare is going on because the rich racists are taking advantage of the poor population.

Actually we should be looking and acting on the real problems stirred by personal greed in government, entertainment, and news media that ignore Christian values.

Every year, I see the boiling pot of violence stirred by political agendas. The values preached aren't working, and they never will, because they are based on fantasy, not fact.

Crime needs to be called crime. And I can tell you that the good people in these communities do not want crime.

Jesus told his followers, "If you hold to my teaching . . . you will know the truth, and the truth will set you free" (John 8:31). If we're missing the truth, that would explain why our values aren't working.

Failure of Violence

After rioting had hit a dozen or so cities, Franklin Graham and his association brought teams of people to work for peace in Charlotte, North Carolina.

He asked, after all the violence had done nothing but harm, why people hadn't yet figured out that it didn't accomplish any good for anyone. We might start with prayer. He encouraged churches, their leaders, and individuals from all denominations to pray. Our problems weren't just political and economic. We were in trouble socially, and we needed God's help.

Perhaps that is the greatest distinction between old-fashioned and modern values. We not only know God exists, but we recognize our need for his help.

Our Eagle Is Ill

If my people, who are called by my name, will humble
themselves and pray and seek my face and turn from their
wicked ways, then I will hear from heaven, and I will forgive
their sin and will heal their land. — *2 Chronicles 7:14*

The bald eagle is our national symbol of strength and success, able to fly high into the clouds. Killing one is illegal, an offense subject to a fine as much as $100,000—in some cases, as much as $250,000. We've passed laws against insecticides that made them sick, so we now have eagles flying in every state. I'd like to see our country flying high again.

"Illegal"—A Sick Bird

I don't understand why many of the politicians ruling our country think breaking the law is not "illegal." Our political pesticides are making our great symbols of strength and success very sick.

I see the news media promoting illegal immigration as being "politically correct." We're being fed poison hidden in something that sounds good. The side-effects could be fatal.

Some people think we need "sanctuary cities" to protect the good people who are breaking the law. Adding criminals to our society, who threaten our freedoms, doesn't seem to be a concern.

We used to be a nation by and for the people. If we didn't like the laws, wisdom prevailed, and we changed the laws. Now, we have this insane sickness that says we only have to obey the laws we like.

I understand that lawmakers are not held in high regard. What I don't understand is why we keep electing people only because we like their charisma and what they say. We won't seriously consider

106

their character, motivation, and experience. If we like them, we don't care if they are crooks.

Illegal Benefits

Would we be concerned if we knew how much of our taxpayer dollars went to support criminals? If we think the rich are paying those taxes, probably not. But we might have second thoughts if we realize that we're paying the rich people's taxes in our high prices for the goods we purchase.

I've paid a lot of taxes in my day, both directly to the government and as a part of purchases. Paying taxes comes with financial success, and I like that. What I don't like is the government waste and paying for the benefits of people who have invaded our country illegally.

I wonder about our politicians in Congress. Don't they understand the meaning of "illegal"? They should. After all, most of them are lawyers. I wonder if we've grown a new breed of lawyers who have learned how to milk the system for political gain, in effect subverting the very laws they are sworn to uphold. Apparently, they don't have my old-fashioned values. They just want enough votes to keep them in power.

Open Borders

The problem with illegal immigration from the south is nothing new. Past administrations have called for a barrier to protect our borders from an onslaught of people who would corrupt our values, be a threat to our society, and receive benefits greater than even our rich country can afford.

Why do some politicians now push so hard against protecting our borders when they once preached its necessity? Something about their values must have changed. Perhaps it's too hard for them to do what's right and then explain their actions to their voters.

Invasion of Privacy

Without proper identification, we can't board an airplane. Threats to our security have made that mandatory. Yet some people think we should be able to vote without anything to identify us as law-abiding citizens. For many, illegal voting isn't seen as a threat to our security.

I often hear claims that these illegal aliens are "hard working people who just want to be part of America." If that's true, then why can't they enter the country legally? If a man entered my house through a side door without knocking, I wouldn't think he just wanted to be part of my family. His illegal presence would say he's more likely a criminal, there for harm, not help.

Asking for identification isn't an invasion of privacy. It's to keep our privacy from being invaded.

Secret Payments

With our credit cards and bank accounts, most of us leave a money trail that investigators could follow if they had a warrant. But the exchange of cash is more difficult to track. No drug lord wants payment by check. When people work for cash, they often do so to avoid paying taxes and having to account for what they do with the money.

No one really knows the number of dollars earned by illegal immigrants working for cash. We do know that this "underground economy" is huge, with much of the money leaving our economy for some foreign country. I once read that $500 billion tax dollars had been lost in a single year from people not paying taxes on their income. That adds up to a lot of illegal behavior.

Illegals have good reason to work for cash. Reporting their incomes could alert authorities about their illegal status, and not paying taxes is a huge benefit. Mr. Joe Legal might make $25 per hour, but he has income tax and Social Security withholding. He pays for insurance, housing, and food at the normal rate. But Mr. Cash has more in his pocket at $15 per hour, because he doesn't pay taxes, gets subsidized housing, and receives food stamps and lunch programs for his children. And good ole Mr. Legal helps pay for those benefits, including the education of Mr. Cash's children.

Path to Citizenship

Our country does not deal with illegal border crossing like we once did. We seem inclined to throw out a welcome mat to everyone.

A tremendous difference exists between those who want to come to our country to enjoy its benefits and those who want to be Americans. Achieving citizenship through our government bureaucracy isn't easy. Some friends of mine came from England. They are highly intelligent, rank among the top wage earners, and have paid their share of taxes. They expended a lot of effort, expense, and patience for about three years before they finally gained citizenship. They almost gave up.

I recall reading about Quang Nguyen, who said the American dream does exist, because he was living it. After eight years of standing in line, he proudly recited the Pledge of Allegiance and became a U.S. citizen. His story was about determination, not entitlement. I think he understands the importance of legal immigration and that valuable things come at significant cost. I'm sure he still holds some love for Vietnam, but he's an American now. We'll not see him marching on the capitol, screaming about how mean and cruel our country is.

The Deceptive Spin

Statistics are so easy to manipulate. You just choose the numbers that support your agenda and ignore what doesn't. What we call journalism today presents mostly opinion pieces, often from a narrow political perspective. "The spin" may support modern values and what people want to believe, but a lack of objective fact-finding and reporting lead people to wrong conclusions.

I heard a newscaster support illegal immigration by citing numbers for how much they spend in this country—supposedly over $10 billion. Where would our economy be if we lost that revenue? Obviously, our country would fare better with more immigrants, not less.

In business, I learned that a company can take in a billion dollars and is sure to go bankrupt if its expenses exceed that amount. The same is true for our country. How much are these immigrants costing the American taxpayer for government support? If we're spending more than we're taking in, it's a bad deal. Could it be enough to bankrupt the country?

I did some research and found several agencies that estimated the taxpayer cost at over $100 billion. That's a 90 percent loss. A closer look said they weren't considering *all* the costs. When those were considered, the estimate soared to $500 billion, a 98 percent loss. Those are round, "ballpark" numbers, and I don't know how accurate they are, but I hope you get the point.

My old-fashioned values worked because we dealt with facts, not the political spinning of statistics. We used to laugh at snake oil salesmen, but now we campaign for them.

The Best Medicine

We could use a healthy dose of old-fashioned law enforcement and respect for our laws. Years ago, we used to enforce the laws without question. Those who didn't were grouped with the criminals, who violated the law. Those lines are now so blurred. I sometimes have trouble distinguishing who we think the wrongdoers are, the lawmakers or the criminals.

Welfare reform may not be a popular topic, but we could use a good dose of that too. If welfare benefits were only paid to people really in need, such as physical and mental cases and short-term unemployment, we could eliminate the incentive to not work. Tax receipts would go up and welfare costs would go down.

E-Verify is a free federal system that allows employers to determine whether new-hires had a legal right to work. Problem is, not everybody uses it. We really need to take that medicine if we want to encourage citizenship and discourage illegal immigration.

Equally enforce federal laws everywhere, eliminate sanctuary cities, and improve the prescriptions for Green Card and Work Visa programs. Eliminate all benefits for illegal immigrants. Treat those who shouldn't be in the country as criminals, not minor offenders.

Establish a path for citizenship that encourages immigrants to learn English, respect our country, and gain legal status.

Nobody seems willing to swallow the truth about having fair taxation. I understand why most people would rather have the *other* person pay their tax burden, but is that fair? If all sales were taxed a small percentage, regardless of product or purchaser, then those who have lots of money and spend a lot would pay the lion's share of tax. And those who had little money would be paying little tax, but it would be their fair share. And then we wouldn't need all the IRS agents, lawyers, and tax accountants to game the system.

If our politicians aren't helping our government's health, we don't need a second opinion. We need a new doctor. Vote the new-fashioned politicians out of office and get old-fashioned leaders who will correctly diagnose and treat the disease instead of telling us to take two aspirin and vote for them again, as if we'll feel better in the morning.

War on Seniors

Even when I am old and gray, do not forsake me, my God, till
I declare your power to the next generation, your mighty acts to
all who are to come. — Psalm 71:18

In our modern world, the problem with seniors is being out-of-touch with the times. They're just too old-fashioned.

A Valuable Old Goose

An old saying advises that we shouldn't kill the goose that lays gold eggs. My old-fashioned values say we don't want to lose the knowledge and wisdom that brought us to where we are, but many think we don't have much to offer anymore.

Since I'm an old goose, I have a different opinion. I am part of a great and wonderful part of our country's population. I thank God every day that I can celebrate being a "senior."

In recent years, we've taken sides in political wars against just about everything: women, children, marriage, race, the environment—even cows—to entitle some voting block to special goodies. Those poor cows. They've been treated so unfairly. I wonder if we'll see a counter-attack.

The Silent Generation

My fellow Americans who were born in the 1930s and 1940s don't complain much. We don't blame others for our hardships.

Social Security didn't even exist until 1935, and we did complain about that 1 percent being withheld from our wages. A government promise of retirement at age 65 didn't mean much when most people didn't live past 60. We didn't make war over it, because we loved our country and could trust most politicians to be honest back then.

Broken Promises

Supposedly, young workers could trust the government to keep our 1 percent, matched with 1 percent from our employer, and keep adding interest over the next forty years. We saw this as our money, wisely invested, that would provide income equal to what we earned while working. Now we know it didn't work out the way we thought it would.

Most seniors have worked hard all of their lives and paid their taxes. They served in the military, and some died for their country. In raising their families, they paid their own way, expecting no government benefits until retirement. When those promises were broken, people didn't have funds to pay their medical bills, and we needed Medicare and Medicaid.

With changes in insurance laws, we expected to keep our doctor. But we soon learned another lesson about broken promises.

Dishonorable Discharge

Years ago, children understood the biblical principle of honoring parents and grandparents. After all, it was item four in the Ten Commandments. But now, we don't want those rules posted in public places, lest someone read them and follow them.

Most seniors don't protest, start riots, or write confrontational blogs. Without their efforts, we wouldn't have the innovations, successes, and freedoms we have today. So I have to wonder if our modern values are taking us in the right direction, where so many children disrespect their parents and adults are so focused on their own possessions and pleasures that they have no concern for seniors.

Marketers are most concerned with who has money to spend. Politicians conduct polls to show where they can get the most votes. Even service organizations can be more concerned with funding to pay salaries and overhead than for helping people. The old saying that the "squeaking wheel gets the grease" can leave seniors feeling like they've been discharged and forgotten.

False Positive

Political promises tell me I have never had it so good. But when I compare life as it is now with what I had without so much government help, I long for the good old days.

I worked very hard for many years to earn the assets I now have, so you might understand why I might resent the new-fashioned values that say I should share with those who don't want to work. Some would have us believe that seniors with that attitude are just being greedy, but it's more a matter of wanting to keep what we've earned. Admittedly, I am old-fashioned, but I don't want my wealth redistributed to anyone other than my heirs.

Politicians may claim to have my best interests at heart, but I see many of their supposedly positive promises to actually be false.

Salute for Past Service

Young men and women in active duty receive significant recognition and social perks, but those who fought in past wars are often forgotten. I served sixteen years in the military, because I loved my country and believed we had freedoms worth fighting for.

Seniors didn't fight in the forgotten wars so they would be recognized, but I do think they deserve something more than a little recognition on Veteran's Day. I think those who weren't in the military but have dedicated many decades to service, promoting the American dream, should get more than a senior discount when they buy something.

Most graduating high school seniors never heard of the Korean War, let alone why it was important. Surely, they should have some understanding of why over a million people died in the Vietnam War, but few do. If people are overlooking seniors who spent most of their lives fighting for our old-fashioned values of religious and social freedom, I fear that this shift in values could bring death to the American dream and healthy, two-parent families.

Respect Your Elders

Sometimes I wonder how many young folks today know about the fifth commandment. With the Ten Commandments no longer posted in public, I suspect the number is small and shrinking.

Those commandments were given to help, not harm us. We need to honor our parents and respect our elders.

Given the number of young people who have little respect for authority, I have to wonder what values are being taught in public schools today. They seem more inclined to protest and riot, wanting to be heard and respected, rather than respect decades of experience and want to hear the wisdom of seniors.

I find it hard to visualize my generation protesting from their wheelchairs and walkers. Maybe we could write more protest blogs and send unfairness messages on Facebook.

My old-fashioned values say I shouldn't waste time complaining. I should respect those in authority, communicate the need as I see it, and vote my convictions at the ballot box.

Inflated Dollars

Seniors are in a battle on several fronts. Some are more obvious than others. For most people active in the workplace, inflation brings a false sense of advancement.

The first federal minimum wage was 25 cents per hour in 1938, when a loaf of bread cost 8 cents, or 32 percent of minimum wage. Twenty years later, that amount had quadrupled to about a dollar. In 2009, it had almost quadrupled twice again, to $7.25 per hour. Now, a loaf of bread costs around $2.50, or 34 percent of minimum wage. As wages go up, so do the cost of goods, and typically, an hour's wage buys just a little less than it used to.

Many seniors in retirement are fighting a battle they can't win, because their savings won't keep up with rising prices.

Deflated Buying Power

A 2 percent inflation rate doesn't sound like much, but that's 2 percent on top of last year's 2 percent. Some years have been 5, 10, even 15 percent. Maybe you've noticed that prices on a grocery item might be about the same for a year or two, then jump 10 percent or more. After going up, the prices seldom go down.

When the government spends more than it takes in, inflation tends to increase and the value of the dollar goes down. I can remember when a dollar would buy what now costs twenty.

Workers who get raises may not be bothered by that, but many seniors are finding that their retirement isn't what they thought it would be.

Those who saved money in low-risk accounts weren't badly hit when the stock market took a dive, but the interest earnings are close to 0 percent, not enough to notice—certainly not enough to keep up with even a 2 percent inflation rate. While others were spending all their earnings, we scrimped and saved money that's now worth less. My paid-up life insurance policies bought with valuable dollars years ago have depreciated so much that they're now nearly worthless.

Affordable Healthcare

Our government has subsidized low interest rates with taxpayer money and the printing of more money. This is great profit for banks, financial institutions, and businesses. Many in top management today receive enormous salaries, bonuses, and benefits including healthcare and life insurance. That's wonderful for them, but for an old executive like me, I get none of that.

The politicians said a change in the healthcare system was for my own good. Millions more Americans would have affordable insurance. To help us see what a wonderful opportunity this was, those who chose not to participate had to pay a penalty.

What it seems to have been is another scheme to take from those who have more and give to those who have less. This is a good political move as long as those who receive free benefits greatly outnumber those who are sacrificing their hard-earned money. I paid handsomely for Medicare benefits all those years, and now I now get less than what was promised. I'm paying more for something I didn't want in the first place. All those deductibles and loopholes in the regulations have left me paying almost $20,000 per year out of my pocket for this affordable healthcare.

In the early years of Medicare, I was told that paying every year while I was young and healthy would cover all my costs when I was older, retired, and needed more healthcare. Maybe we should go back to my old-fashioned values when we didn't trust snake oil remedies, used car salesmen, or the razzle-dazzle words of politicians.

116

"Free" at High Cost

We seniors didn't just now walk in out of the rain. When something is labeled free for the majority of the voting public, we don't need a magnifying glass to read the small print. We already know what it says. We'll be paying more so others can have "free."

Whenever the government wants to offer more free benefits to a large block of voters, they have to take from whoever has money. Or they just print more money, which boosts inflation. Either way, we're paying the bill.

I never liked paying Social Security, because I didn't believe the promises. I paid into this "insurance" fund for some fifty years, knowing I would need to fund my own retirement. But now that I have more money, my benefits are less. I confess, I don't like my Social Security payments touted as "your government benefit," as if I'm being given something I've not already paid for.

Allies

Some people and agencies really do care about seniors like me. For example, we have AARP representing us in Washington. I like AARP a lot, but even nonprofits can't function if they spend more than they take in. Therefore, seniors are their concern, but only after they look out for themselves.

Because people are so tied to the screen these days, the media could do a lot to improve society's regard for seniors, but I'm not seeing much positive support. Articles often question our mental capacity, our ability to drive, and our old-fashioned values, as if we are some kind of drain on society.

I'm sorry, but my values don't let me sit around and play with the latest gadgets.

Fine Print

I admit, my eyes don't focus as well as when I was young, but I don't think it's my imagination. The fine print has now become even smaller. I can remember when the type on a medicine bottle was large enough to read, but now? I need to carry a magnifying glass into the drugstore to read the labels.

I must now renew my driver's license in person, just to be sure I can still read the road signs and I appear to still be someone who can drive safely. I don't drink and drive. I don't do drugs. You'll never see me texting or talking on my cell phone. I've never had an accident, and I've never been fined for reckless driving. Isn't that what all the young folks do? Maybe they should be the ones taking the tests, not me.

Winnable War

The war is over when we surrender, and I hope seniors will never quit fighting for the values that served us well for centuries. We're not ones to protest or riot, and we may be tired, but we shouldn't even think about giving up.

Seniors may be criticized for being old-fashioned and not believing political rhetoric, but we have value that can't be found anywhere else. Our eight to ten decades of experience is a treasure that should never be lost.

Our voice can still be heard—if we speak up.

Not Our Fault

Upon reflection, I must point out that seniors did *not* take . . .

- The melody out of music,
- The pride out of appearance,
- The courtesy out of driving,
- The romance out of love,
- The commitment out of marriage,
- The responsibility out of parenthood,
- The togetherness out of the family.
- The learning out of education,
- The service out of patriotism,
- The Golden Rule from rulers,
- The nativity scene out of cities,
- The civility out of behavior,
- The refinement out of language,
- The dedication out of employment,

118

- The prudence out of spending,
- The ambition out of achievement, or
- God out of government and public education.

We certainly are *not* the ones who eliminated patience and tolerance from personal relationships and interactions with others. We won't march on Washington or riot in our walkers. We won't hit people with our canes.

Smaller Inheritance

To add insult to injury, the war does not stop when I die. As I lay peacefully in my casket, the government would like to have everything I leave on Earth. Some politicians seem to believe the government is owed the fruits of my labor because they gave me the opportunity to be successful.

Young people need to be aware that the battle continues, because the youth of today will become the seniors of tomorrow.

New-Fashioned Dependency

We gave you this rule: "The one who is unwilling to work shall not eat." We hear that some among you are idle and disruptive. . . . Such people we command and urge in the Lord Jesus Christ to settle down and earn the food they eat.
— 2 Thessalonians 3:10–12

One of my biggest values is that my government and I should help those who cannot help themselves—and we should be very generous. But that should not include the people who don't want to work.

Freeloaders

I am tired of supporting freeloaders who want me to pay for their unwillingness to work. Judging by the apostle Paul's words, I don't think God thinks very highly of moochers either.

Things have changed a lot since I started working at the age of nine and had a bank account at age ten. I was able to pay for my own stuff. When I married and had children, I had dependents to declare on my tax return. I gladly accepted responsibility for supporting my family. In the 1960s, I learned that my taxes were supporting a lot of people other than those claimed on my tax return.

The Great Society

Under President Lyndon Johnson, the government introduced programs that were supposed to eliminate poverty and social injustice. I was being asked to support many others who needed help because they were poorer than me. We were told that it was

120

the right thing to do. Many people thought that was a good idea—especially those who would receive benefits without paying anything for them.

At first, I didn't feel too bad about that. But when my taxes kept rising, I began to wonder where my hard-earned money was going. Besides my own family, how many dependents was I expected to support?

In the 1970s, our family moved to New Jersey, and I worked in New York City, where I paid exorbitant property and capital gains taxes in New Jersey, New York, and New York City—on top of what I had to pay in federal taxes. Evidently, one of the most prosperous areas of the country had a lot of poverty.

New York City seemed to have an awful lot of people who were entitled to my support because they were disadvantaged. What they were receiving for not working wasn't enough, because they protested in front of NBC, across the street from my office. And that got a lot of news coverage. Obviously, the government wasn't doing enough for them.

The Great Society failed miserably in reaching its goals. Instead of getting better, conditions have worsened. I think we'd be better off with more of our old-fashioned values.

Unequal Opportunity

When my daughter graduated from a large high school, second in her class, I learned that her chance for a college scholarship was close to zero. The quotas for the "less fortunate" students had to be filled first. Her academic merits didn't matter. She wasn't poor enough to qualify.

Somehow, others were more entitled to a scholarship, even though I paid local, state, and federal taxes. To get her degree, she ended up working to pay most of her way. The Great Society provided an unequal opportunity, helping dependents outside my family, but not my daughter.

Nowhere to Run

Like many others who needed to solve this dependency problem, we moved away from the New York City area. But we couldn't escape all the high state and federal taxes.

Not only do I receive no thanks for paying high taxes, I hear that I'm not paying enough. The rich are seen as not paying their fair share, because others are entitled to more. As my unidentified dependents become more demanding, protestors may riot or march on Washington, and politicians will cheer them on.

Shrinking Assets

In retirement, I have only my wife and myself to support, yet the government seems intent on taking a larger share of my hard-earned investment income every year.

It's not just federal taxes that support dependencies. I get to pay increased costs for healthcare, school taxes, license fees, and sales taxes to support more and more "dependents."

I shudder to think what will happen in a few years, after we've added many millions of illegal immigrants to our welfare rosters. At some point, either the rich people will run out of money. Or the rich might leave the country.

Increasing Dependencies

As a member of The Heritage Foundation, I receive publications that say a lot about what is happening in our country. As our population is increasing, the percentage of people who pay federal income taxes is decreasing. Social Security benefits are more than the taxes collected each year, and Medicare collections won't meet expenses either.

I wonder how people believe the government can give away even more free stuff. We may not be far from a socialist government that wants all our money so it can decide who should get what. If we can't return to some of our old-fashioned values, I fear that we'll be unable to pull back from the brink of complete dependence on government.

Taxation without Representation

With more and more people not paying, fewer and fewer votes exist to vote against higher taxes. If we consider the huge percentage of people who either work for the government or receive free benefits, we might understand why politicians are free to promote bigger government with the enticement of more "free" benefits.

I wonder what would happen if only taxpaying citizens were allowed to vote on whether to increase taxes. Don't assume we would vote against taxes, because that's not the case. But we would demand a balanced budget in which we can be sure the money isn't being wasted, doesn't finance political perks, and goes to real needs, not to those who just don't want to work.

Growing Voter Dependence

Dependence-creating programs are assets that many of our politicians will embrace with gusto. The people electing these supposedly good-hearted leaders tend to vote in response to promises of higher wages and increased benefits. Once initiated, these programs keep adding dependence, increasing the national debt and the financial burden of the minority who pay taxes.

Since government jobs are easier, pay higher wages, get lucrative pensions, and give raises based on tenure, not productivity, workers have an incentive to leave the private sector and work for the government, which increases the voter base that wants a socialist administration.

Broken Promises

After being promised the moon, some retirees will be really upset when their bankrupt city governments can't fund their pensions. We've already seen that happen, and it will get worse if we continue our new-fashioned mindset that the government can give us all we want.

For almost two hundred years, no one had ever heard of government-subsidized housing. But in 1965, our government founded the U.S. Department of Housing and Urban Development (HUD) with its thousands of employees and an annual budget that has grown to over $25 billion. This program was to bring peace and harmony to our communities, because we assumed that rioting and crime came from poverty and poor housing. But actually, this huge addition to the taxpayer burden hasn't delivered on its promises.

Subsidized Farming

My married life began with farming. My parents and grandparents never heard of government subsidies. I first saw them in the mid-1950s. With the supply exceeding demand, prices were plummeting, and the revenue wouldn't cover our expenses.

Organizers stirred up the farmers with the idea of "parity," a means for the government to guarantee prices at a profitable level. Farmers joined to form a lobby. In those days, there were still enough voting farmers to get politicians' attention. My neighbor, Oran Lee Staley, became president of the National Farmers Organization (NFO). Their national meetings were huge. Celebrity entertainers came to support the poor farmer's plight. Politicians gave thundering speeches that made national news. It was a powerful movement because of the number of votes involved.

Next came the "soil banks," which were programs to pay farmers to take their land out of production. What a deal, getting paid *not* to work. My old-fashioned values said all these free benefits were actually going to raise costs, not reduce them. Prices and taxes were sure to go up.

The production of ethanol from corn and other plant materials was encouraged as a great benefit. Farmers had a new source of income, but at what cost to the public? Without government subsidies, it wouldn't be much. What I see are higher prices at the grocery story, and I have my doubts whether we've done much to curb global warming.

Farm subsidies have become one of America's largest welfare programs. I've seen real estate ads saying you could buy the farm and make money by doing nothing but take the soil-bank subsidy.

I knew that somebody had to pay for everything that was free, and somewhere in all the hidden costs, I'd be paying too. I'm thankful that I left that business before I too became a government dependent.

Food Stamps

The first food stamps came off the printing presses in 1939, but it was nothing like what we have today. Like with most government welfare programs, the number of people who benefit and the costs to the taxpayer has seen out-of-control growth for most of the last seventy years.

Instead of "food stamps," we now have SNAP, an acronym for the Supplemental Nutrition Assistance Program, an important change in our age of political correctness. One out of five families depends on this program to put food on the table.

Healthcare

The industry has so much government intervention, it's no wonder that costs are so high and the system is so badly broken. Medicare and Medicaid are huge champions of government dependency. Like Social Security, the true cost is hidden. For decades, people pay withholding for benefits they will never collect if they die before they turn sixty-five.

What happens to the federal withholding for all the years while young employees are paying insurance and medical costs in addition? The money funds the dependency of older folks who are currently eligible for benefits, because the government spent their past withholding long ago.

I hear talk that we should have Medicare for all ages, which is a good political ploy since it appeals to a very large block of voters. The expense would be astronomical, but that seems to be overlooked. Where would those dollars come from? As our dependency on government increases, get ready for more hidden costs and higher taxes.

Expanded Welfare

The 1996 Welfare Reform Act replaced the decades-long Aid to Families with Dependent Children (AFDC), a cash program to provide financial assistance to needy dependent children. Once established, that program swelled to include unemployed parents of enrolled children. As state welfare rolls increased, more and more taxpayer money was allocated.

What I'm sure were good intentions led to some really bad incentives. The welfare opportunity discouraged able-bodies adults from working and being married. Many found ways to lie and cheat the system.

The 1996 Act made benefits temporary and encouraged people to find work. But under the Obama administration, those reforms disappeared. States received cash bonuses for growing their welfare rolls, and they did. Incentive to work and be self-sufficient reached an all-time low.

Cradle-to-grave welfare has produced the largest class of non-working people in the history of our country. When the government will support your children and pay for their education, including college, why work?

Education

As we have become more dependent on government to provide education, costs have risen much more than our rate of inflation. I don't know how accurate the statistics are, but I've read that, compared to when I was in school, we have four times the staff for 25 percent less enrollment. I'm all for improving the quality of education, but our new-fashioned values don't seem to be working.

Government Jobs

In all levels of government—federal, state, and local—we need more and more employees to administer all the programs. We now have more people working for the government than for all the Fortune 500 companies combined, making it the biggest "business" in the world.

We should feel blessed to have children and grandchildren as our dependents, but I have to wonder if all the government programs will keep them from getting a reasonable share of my inheritance. I'm not sure I can afford many more dependents. I sure don't get to claim them on my income tax returns.

A Question of Value

The greatest among you will be your servant. For those who exalt themselves will be humbled, and those who humble themselves will be exalted. — Matthew 23:11–12

Few young people today know who our thirty-fifth president was, but if they paid attention in their American History classes, they just might know about his famous words in his inaugural address. "Ask not what your country can do for you. Ask what you can do for your country." With those words, he challenged our nation's values. Should we be a society focused on giving or getting?

Today's Focus

Politicians today don't say much about what people should give. If they want to raise taxes, they talk about the rich paying more, not that we ourselves should have an attitude for giving. We mostly hear promises of what the government will give us if we vote for that candidate.

In 1961, President Kennedy's words resonated with many, because we could see our society drifting toward self-centered greed for all the government should give them. Our strong feeling of patriotism was fading, and we knew continuing in that direction would not be good. We didn't want to lose our old-fashioned values centered on giving for the good of our country and the benefit of all Americans.

Today, President Kennedy's words would not be politically acceptable in either party, Democrat or Republican. That's because most people aren't interested in what they can do for their country. They don't even want to know what they can do for themselves.

They are asking what the government can do for them, the very thing our president warned against.

Many of my fellow Americans think of Uncle Sam as their rich uncle who never runs out of money or goodies to give them. Education should be free. Healthcare should be free. We should all be given high-paying jobs that aren't too demanding. If we don't want to work or can't find a job, that suits us. The government should give us housing, food, and enough to pay our bills.

In the last sixty years, our values have changed drastically.

Age of Entitlement

So far, so good. Maybe. As long as government can print up money and redistribute it, all the beneficiaries will be happy. Since so many other governments have tried that and failed, I'm not sure how much longer we can go without a balanced budget before our dollars become worthless.

The fastest growing segments of our population are those receiving benefits from the government, and most people who are struggling to make it on their own expect more government help. Why? The single-word answer is "entitlement." The media and politicians keep promoting the idea that we're being mistreated in some way. If it's not race, it's religion. If not that, then it's another form of social prejudice. Stirring anger among different groups that we're not getting our "fair share" improves television ratings, boosts traffic on social networks, and helps politicians get elected.

The more that people hear that college should be free, the more they feel cheated when they have to pay. Many people now expect retirement security even if they've paid little, if anything, into the Social Security fund. Because of the entitlement concept, people think the homeless communities exist only because the government isn't doing enough. They see the government as a rich uncle who isn't taking care of them, not giving them their fair share.

Our new-fashioned values say the minimum wage should be doubled, but prices shouldn't go up. Taxing the rich, forcing them to pay their "fair share," will pay for food stamps, subsidized housing, and free education and healthcare. With my old-fashioned values, I know that entitlement expectation is an absolute impossibility.

128

Never Enough

The apostle Paul said, "Godliness with contentment is great gain" (1 Timothy 6:6). I'm afraid that our new-fashioned values will eventually take us to the unavoidable flipside to that truth, which says, "Ungodliness with discontent is great loss."

For almost two centuries after this nation was established, our old-fashioned values recognized our need to respect God's Word, strive to do our best, and be thankful and content with God's provision. I fear that those who still feel that way today are a dying breed. Our society promotes such a high level of discontent and disbelief in God, I believe that our values must change or people will never have enough. They will never be content.

Free Stuff

We like free stuff as long as we can believe it's really free. At one time, "buy one, get one free" was a great promotional ploy until people realized it was just a 50 percent discount on inflated prices. Now, we see more advertised discounts and special prices. When something is free, we want to know why, but not always. Somehow, our value system changes when the government is making the offer.

Those who get the free stuff from the government are happy, because somebody else is paying. They think the rich taxpayers wouldn't be so rich if they were paying their fair share. Wanting more free stuff, they resent the taxpayers who have so much.

The taxpayers are frustrated because they scrimped and saved, worked very hard, and took financial risks but don't have enough to show for their effort. As soon as they became successful, the government took more of their money to pay for all the free stuff for others. They don't like their hard-earned money being taken from them so unsuccessful, sometimes lazy, people can have more.

Politicians get votes by promising more free stuff than they can possibly deliver. They use their power and prestige to put themselves among the rich elite while condemning those who worked so hard for their success as being uncaring, prejudiced, and racist.

Easy Credit

When I was young, borrowing was only possible with sufficient assets to guarantee that the lender wouldn't suffer an unrecoverable loss. But now, as long as the consumer keeps making the minimum payment on a credit card, the total debt can quickly rise to $50,000 or more—and keep rising—until the debtor can't pay at all. When the amount is "written off," the remaining credit card holders must cover the loss in the exorbitant interest rates.

Our new-fashioned values accept government debt like a credit card with a limit in the trillions of dollars, which can be raised as soon as we want to spend trillions more. Politicians aren't likely to be elected if they say we need to curtail spending and balance the budget. What has happened to our sense of values?

I'm afraid our easy credit can't last forever. The next generation might face a tax burden that would take almost all their earnings and destroy people's incentive to work.

Productivity

In the old days, we believed in a reward for our labor. If we wanted a great harvest, we had to plow the fields, sow the seed, and pray for rain. We didn't expect life to be easy, because we believed our success depended upon how hard we were willing to work. That doesn't seem to be as true today.

Now, too many people are looking for easy money. For some, that means selling drugs or prostitution. For others, welfare works. Young people might go to college on student loans they'll never be able to repay, expecting a management position as soon as they graduate, believing they will make six figures at a nine-to-four job. Few people want to start at the bottom and slowly work their way up the corporate ladder. That was what we did in the old-fashioned days.

I've read estimates that about 5 percent of the homeless have college degrees. I don't know how accurate that number is, but the fact that it's anything above a tenth of 1 percent makes me question our modern values. Apparently, many people no longer understand the value of work.

Technology

We no longer use horse-drawn plows. Cassette tapes and typewriters are obsolete. Our machines with artificial intelligence are replacing the work we used to do by hand, so now we need only check to be sure everything is running satisfactorily. With computers building computers, we're producing more and more with less and less work by human hands. I wonder how these changes are affecting our values, the quality of our lives, and our feelings of self-worth.

With all our social networking, we seem to be isolating ourselves. While preaching inclusion, we've developed a new talent for excluding all who don't agree with us. Instead of freedom of religion, we practice freedom *from* religion. We would rather protest what we lack instead of being thankful for our blessings.

If we could return to some of our old-fashioned values, we might see our American flag flying proudly instead of having so many people wanting to burn it.

Values Cycle

Over the hundreds of years of Jewish history, generations progressed toward and away from God in predictable cycles. The Bible tells us about people making sacrifices to idols in the Temple that was once filled with God's glory (1 Kings 8:10–11; 2 Kings 23:4). When the ways of the world look good to us, we easily drift away from the divine principles that gave us life.

In past millennia, great kingdoms appeared to be invincible until they fell. Our nation was founded on biblical principles that voters supported, and it appears to be invincible, but is it really? With our changing values, maybe not.

More and more voters look to the government, not God, to meet their needs. They elect political candidates like children who've been offered candy. As the tax burden increases, fewer and fewer people have a desire to work. Eventually the economic system cannot sustain itself, and the socialist society bows to a dictator.

In colonial times, the persecuted in Europe fled to America for religious freedom and to escape the peasant society that left few opportunities for success. From faith came courage, which led to freedom and opportunity that brought abundance. That success encouraged an entitlement mentality that promoted ignorance and apathy, which led to the dependencies that are taking us into the bondage and persecutions that our ancestors fled.

If we want to break the vicious cycle, we will have to return to many of our old-fashioned, biblical values.

Ignorance and Apathy

A college student was asked which he thought was the greater problem in our society, ignorance or apathy. As the man shrugged and walked away, he said, "I don't know, and I don't care."

We face a crisis that has plenty of people alarmed, but the majority of young Americans either don't know or don't care. Maybe both. They can't admit there is a problem with spending more than you take in. They won't add the numbers, because they'd rather believe in magic than face reality.

Some people see crises looming and want to curb the entitlement mentality and reduce our dependency of government. But popular politicians fight cutbacks, wanting to spend more, not less. They say our government would collapse if its dependents lost their benefits.

Ignorance allows people to believe the lie that taxpayers are greedy, unwilling to share, if they ever complain about paying more tax. Ignorance allows people to believe businesses take advantage of their employees, not paying enough, when they should appreciate the prosperous enterprises that want more workers and will pay more for better skills and improved performance.

The Vocal Minority

To be heard, grab the microphone and captivate an audience. No keynote speaker ever gained celebrity by preaching to the mirror or taking the stage before a packed room of empty chairs.

"Equalize the wealth" sounds really good to the multitude who will receive the benefits. Politicians who champion that message hold the microphone and gather crowds like rodents entranced by the Pied Piper's tune.

Who really benefits from the microphone message? Not the multitude, but the few who hold the microphones and promote the new-fashioned values. Government leaders and a circle of friends and relatives acquire tremendous wealth while the crowds keep cheering for more benefits like the proverbial carrot that eternally dangles before the horse's nose.

I wish old-fashioned values could grab a microphone and hold the attention of the crowd that needs to hear the message. We should at least try to avoid being part of a "silent majority."

The Isms

So what about capitalism, socialism and other isms? People's attitudes toward capitalism and free enterprise seem to favor more government control. Millennials and young graduates enter the workforce with a negative view of the freedoms we once held dear. A majority identify with socialist values that the older generations viewed as a threat to our society.

Now, more and more socialist practices are being welcomed as a necessary part of society. A few decades ago, socialist politicians would have been laughed at, but now large crowds applaud them and don't question their promises. This change makes me wonder what children are being taught in school. They can't be hearing what I learned from history about the failures of communism, fascism, and socialism.

In support of the socialist views of many youth, the media gives lavish praise for the communist governments of Cuba and South American countries while ignoring the poverty, failing economies, and oppression of their citizens. In our own country, we cry for more government control and welfare to curb the homelessness, violence, and crime that plagues our society.

Politicians push for more government-run programs and businesses, and too many of our young people haven't been taught enough history to recognize why that might be a problem. When university professors bash the unfairness of capitalism and free enterprise, we can be sure that students aren't hearing the truth about the isms.

Socialism means production to satisfy human needs, not as under capitalism for sale and profit. The government manages all industries and social services.

Communism wants all our production to be owned in common rather than by individuals. In practice, a single authoritarian party controls both the political and economic systems.

Capitalism is characterized by private or corporate ownership of goods through investments made by individuals. Prices, production, and the distribution of goods are determined by competition in a free market, not through government control.

If I were to ask students just out of college to describe socialism, they would most likely say it's the government giving us all the nice things we need—protection for the environment, curbing carbon emissions, and health care and wealth for everyone—everyone "living together equally." What a wonderful dream, but in practice, it doesn't work.

Anyone with my old-fashioned values knows that the more government control we have, the less competition exists—so the rich get richer and the poor get poorer.

When I started making and investing money at age nine, I could barely spell *capitalism*. I didn't know what the word meant, but I loved the opportunity of free enterprise. Later, when I worked very hard to be successful in business, our system allowed me to excel as I never dreamed possible as a child. I really loved that capital "ism" system.

How to Spell Success

Our country has become the most successful country in the world in creating wealth and the highest standard of living for common people.

For the last hundred years, we have been the most powerful defender of freedoms for the world. We have been the most charitable nation. More here than anywhere else, the average child has been free to dream, and with a lot of dedication and hard work, they can see those dreams fulfilled.

What will the next hundred years look like? I fear for what my grandchildren, great-grandchildren, and their children will face if the present trend away from old-fashioned values is allowed to continue. If we let socialism spell success for us, we could suffer the greatest social and economic collapse in history, becoming like the countries that immigrants have fled.

Union leadership has taught members that businesses are greedy, profiting from the backbreaking effort of their employees. They blame the evil corporations for taking manufacturing jobs to other countries. If more people would investigate why that has happened, we might know that corporations aren't evil in making those moves. They do it to remain competitive, to survive all the government regulations and union contracts. Right-to-work states have prospered because of their ability to compete with foreign markets.

Unions are among the largest political contributors. With their large bloc of voters, especially among government workers, they lead the strongest lobbyist groups. Politicians cater to the union influence and spread the same message that the decline in jobs is the fault of evil corporations.

With the badmouthing of capitalism, we're not doing very well at spelling success.

Capitalism

You, my brothers and sisters, were called to be free.
But do not use your freedom to indulge the flesh; rather,
serve one another humbly in love. — Galatians 5:13

When over half the population depends on the government for support, either from work or from welfare, we've already given up much of our opportunity for free enterprise. For every security we get from the government, we've had to give up a portion of our freedom.

Real Business

Most people have never owned a business to know what it's like to live under the burden of government regulation, insurance requirements, and taxation with only the hope that they can provide a product or service that provides more income than expense. Those who have faced those challenges know firsthand what "real business" is all about.

A large segment of our population doesn't do much work, depending on government benefits—welfare, child support, and food stamps. They often view businesses as greedy, unwilling to pay decent wages, unwilling to hire any but the most qualified for the job. They don't think about all the businesses that file for bankruptcy each year because they couldn't get enough income to cover all their expenses. The surviving businesses aren't evil for making a profit. Without them, we would have no jobs in the private sector. The only work available would be for the government.

People who dislike our country should move to a socialist country and learn firsthand how much worse their lives would be.

They should try Cuba's healthcare that is free only if you are fortunate enough to find a doctor who can see you. They should go to a country where the average monthly wage is no more than what most American workers earn in an hour. They might try Greece, where so many are looking for work but can't find anything, and if they should be fortunate to have a job, they pay sky-high taxes.

I believe it was Winston Churchill who once said the main vice of capitalism was the uneven distribution of prosperity, and the main vice of socialism was the even distribution of misery. Under capitalism, all have an opportunity to prosper, some to a greater degree than others. Under socialism, nobody has enough.

Politicians talk about raising taxes on businesses and rich individuals, as if that increase isn't costing us, that the average voter isn't paying anything more. I wish we weren't so gullible, either unable or unwilling to see that real business has no choice but to pass increased costs on to the consumer.

To survive, real business has to cut back somewhere, closing locations, reducing the workforce, or outsourcing to foreign countries.

Rules and Regulations

Regulation on top of regulation has been piled on businesses. For years, our corporate tax rate has been among the highest of the world's industrial nations. As soon as we see just a little relief to boost the economy, politicians excite voters with the prospect of benefits paid by increasing taxes and the national debt.

Besides the federal and state governments, businesses must comply with all the city ordinances and licensing requirements. With all the regulations in New York City, you might take years and a lot of money before you could get all the approvals necessary to open a lemonade stand. The problem reaches from coast to coast. I've read claims that California is by far the worst place to open a new business unless you have a huge bucket full of cash.

The economic cost of regulations laid upon business runs into the hundreds of billions of dollars. If you think businesses are paying those costs, guess again. Yes, they must pay the bills, but the costs are passed on to consumers. We're paying for all the regulations.

Some regulations are good, providing safety and quality of service. We need those regulations, but too many times the restrictions go beyond reason, fees are excessive, and the motivation is to hide what actually amounts to another tax.

Job Creation

Ask the average young person on the street, "Who creates jobs in our country?" Setting aside the blank stares and statements of not knowing or not caring, you'll most likely hear, "The government." They say that because that's what they've heard, and school didn't teach them how our economic system works.

New businesses need employees and will post "Now Hiring" signs. As they prosper and grow, they need more employees who in turn spend money on goods and services, causing other companies to grow. Any company with a desire to prosper and grow is creating more jobs.

When the government increases taxes and adds regulation, business growth is restrained, cutting jobs, increasing unemployment, and causing more people to need government support—which may be "fixed" by increasing taxes and adding to the national debt, cutting even more jobs.

Competition

Capitalism has worked in our country because of its competitive nature. Think of it like a race in which the best will win. Others will do well, and some will drop out. The best businesses win and continue to win until some upstart company has a better product or service, or a lower price. The winners of today can be the losers of tomorrow, and vice-versa. Our country has thrived on these old-fashioned values for centuries.

Our new-fashioned values overlook our need for winners and losers. Not wanting anyone to feel bad about losing, every runner receives a trophy. We think we've done well by not having losers, but actually we've hurt everyone by not having true winners. Those who finished first have less incentive to do better, and those who finished last can be content where they are. We've just described the socialist philosophy that we endorse in government, schools, and the workplace.

Many of my college professor friends couldn't understand why a "smart" person like me would be involved in a "trade." Already they were thinking capitalism was bad and government was good, perhaps because they were comfortable in their professions that largely depended on government support, where there was no risk of losing. Everybody got a prize.

I've experienced both the agony of defeat and the thrill of victory, and I can tell you that both are essential in a healthy economy. Those with socialist values should thank me, because without my taxes and charitable giving made possible in capitalism, they would be looking for work.

Social Inequality

The idea that rich people should be forced to share the wealth has become a big topic in our society. Great advertising makes us want all the things we don't have, and the entitlement message we hear so frequently says we should have them. We look to government like a big brother who will force the bully to share his toys.

What will happen when the government takes over and runs our businesses? The bully won't have any toys, and neither will we. After decades of doing without, some socialist countries have realized that they will have to become more capitalistic to enjoy the kind of prosperity we have had for two hundred years.

In my career, I have led companies in the creation of thousands upon thousands of new jobs, with a lot of personal wealth for employees and shareholders. We need that old-fashioned kind of social inequality. Those would be good values to have today.

Greedy People

Are all business people good? Of course not, but the ones who are bad are soon discovered and have to leave the market to those who are. The wonderful thing about capitalism is the necessity of serving others, delivering a valuable product or service. Without that, a business cannot survive for long. A good competitor will step up and take over.

139

On the other hand, I'm worried about the politicians, lobbyists, and special interests in government, because they seem to be able to get away with just about anything as long as they have significant media and audience support. In the old days, nobody would even think about attacking the president, but now it's the stylish, acceptable thing to do. Many key people in government agencies appear to be greedier than anyone in business ever thought to be. Perhaps we need to apply some old-fashioned values that would make them accountable to the people.

Government-Run Business

For to us a child is born, to us a son is given, and the
government will be on his shoulders. And he will be called
Wonderful Counselor, Mighty God, Everlasting Father,
Prince of Peace. — Isaiah 9:6

The quality of mail service has often been assigned this motto:
"Neither snow nor rain nor heat nor gloom of night stays these
couriers from the swift completion of their appointed rounds." It
hasn't always worked that way, but people accepted the message as
representative of the government's good intentions.

Good Only for a While

How many times have we been told the government had something
good for us, and it turned out to be not-so-good? More than a few,
I think.

Many people want more government control—to run more
businesses and provide healthcare and social benefits. I don't agree,
because I've lived enough to see how political promises are
fulfilled. Invariably, what we're told will save us money actually
drives costs up.

The U.S. Postal Service satisfied some essential needs in the
beginning, but now it's one of the most inefficient, expensive
enterprises in our nation. Without the space program of the 1960s,
we wouldn't have had the rapid growth of computer technology,
but now we're seeing private companies put satellites in orbit at less
expense. In the long run, government services seem always to cost
more.

Customer Service

Back in the old days when people knew the value of work, government employees were more concerned for helping those they served. I still remember when the postal motto was true. Rain, sleet, or snow couldn't keep the postman from his appointed rounds. A first-class letter cost three cents, and I could mail a postcard for a penny. Postal employees were the most highly regarded people in town, because we knew they cared.

Our new-fashioned values have brought better efficiency because of technology, while at the same time service has declined because so many government employees care more for their big paycheck, with less concern for the people they serve. These days, I enjoy going to the post office about as much as visiting the dentist for a root canal. It's painful, time-consuming, and expensive.

Self-Service

I remember when I could pull into a gas station, pay an attendant two dollars, and leave with the tank half full, more air in the tires if needed, and the oil and radiator checked—all without getting out of the car. Those were old-fashioned service values. Now, we pump our own gas, find our own merchandise in the hardware store, and use the self-checkout kiosk. Finding someone eager to help us can be a challenge.

When I go to the post office to mail something or buy stamps, I wait in a long line for maybe twenty minutes. Clerks shuffle in and out without looking up, apparently unaware that I exist. I would say they need more staff to handle peak hours, but actually I think they need people who care about customer service, who don't walk around like robots on the last charge of a dying battery.

Since I face similar problems with other government agencies, I think the lack of service is not as much the people as it is the way that government does business. If I must renew my driver's license in person, I can wait for hours for my number to be called. That's right, we have a system to manage slow service.

On most days, I receive mail, but I never know when that will be. Sometimes, it's ten o'clock in the morning, but it could be after dinner in the evening. I can't complain about late delivery or lost mail, because getting action from anyone in postal management is next to impossible. The only thing harder is getting help from the IRS.

In most cases, if I can't serve myself, I get no service.

Retailing Services

For most of my business career, I have worked at serving customers in the retail markets. If we gave great customer service, our business was rewarded with sales and profits. If we hadn't done that, our business would inevitably fail.

With its multi-billion-dollar losses each year, the U.S. Postal Service should have been out of business long ago—except the government seems willing to allow unlimited losses and deficits. We can be thankful for UPS and FedEx competition. If the USPS had a monopoly on package delivery, we could expect poorer service at much higher prices.

If we compare the USPS profit-and-loss statements with UPS and FedEx, two of the world's most respected and prosperous companies, we don't need to be a genius to see that the government-run company is so poorly managed. It will never be able to compete with retail services in the private sector and operate in the black.

Problem Companies

Part of my business career involved problem companies that were headed for bankruptcy. I know a lot about what a failing business must do to survive and why businesses are driven into bankruptcy.

Our USPS is a classic example of a "problem company." They have had incredibly bad management stoked with cronyism, political favors, and political correctness. Waste and corruption has been covered up and ignored.

Problem companies blame everything and everyone except themselves for their shortcomings. They often let unions dictate work requirements, productivity standards, and basically how the business will be run. Contract negotiations for salaries and retirement packages often put the company at a competitive disadvantage with nonunion companies in right-to-work states.

Contracting work for the federal government adds another layer of restrictions on top of union and state regulations. Any glitch in satisfying government requirements can bankrupt a company with uncollectible receivables.

Bailouts

No business should be too big to fail, because our effort to keep them from failing often results in even greater losses. Is that a big deal? Absolutely, because the consumer ultimately has to cover the loss through more taxes and higher prices.

Suppose a bank loans $10 million to a startup business that is struggling. To keep from having to show a loss, the bank might keep loaning more millions until eventually the business folds, creating a ripple effect like a boulder dropped into a pond, sending the loss all the way to the consumer.

In 2008, the government allocated some $700 billion to keep businesses and financial institutions afloat. Under our old-fashioned values, this would never have been a problem, because banks wouldn't have made so many bad loans and businesses would have failed much earlier, and at much less cost.

Non-service Attitudes

The unions never took the haircuts to salvage their sinking ships. We suckers just keep on listening to the politicians who insist on perpetuating the failures of badly managed organizations. With union and government protection, workers feel secure in their positions, so they don't have to worry about serving customers.

Managers fritter away cash on silly advertising, as if an entertaining image on television is all they need to offset inefficiencies and poor customer service. When the USPS has a monopoly on mailing first-class letters, advertising to make us feel good about paying more for postage makes no sense. Taxpayers don't need that advertising expense.

Without government support and our taxpayer dollars, the USPS could not survive with a ratio of revenue to labor cost that is more than twice as high as UPS and FedEx. I don't see how the USPS losses can continue year after year.

One day, we'll have to face the reality that our new-fashioned values of government control don't work. When we do, that truth may come at a very high cost.

The Blame Game

If we didn't have email, then more people would be writing letters and paying postage. If we didn't have Internet advertising, companies would pay the USPS for mass delivery of fliers and postcards. The private business sector has to adjust for changing technology and consumer practices. But government-businesses don't face the same pressure to change, because they can have the taxpayer support their losses and continue the blame without making changes.

UPS and FedEx do not have a monopoly that would allow high prices and poor service. With no one to blame, they thrive by making adjustments that keep them competitive and prosperous, which a government-run business seems unable to do.

The Solution

Is bankruptcy an option for a government-run business? Probably not. Can the gigantic debts be written off? We have no entities that could sustain such losses. Release from the exorbitant labor contracts and unrealistic pension payouts would help. We could add the ability to fire low-performance employees. Could we have managers from the private sector, who know how business should be run, instead of political appointees? These are the things that could or should happen, but they probably won't.

The USPS provides a needed service. It could be a profitable competitive business with lower prices and better service. With my proven experience, I could fix their problems, but no one like me will be given that opportunity, not in our politically driven system.

That leaves us with only one possible solution. Turn over government-run business to private enterprise where the successful thrive and the unsuccessful are allowed to fail.

Those old-fashioned values built America to be the richest nation in the world. But if our new-fashioned values are allowed to prevail, it could one day become the poorest.

Business Principles

Whoever walks in integrity walks securely, but whoever takes crooked paths will be found out. — *Proverbs 10:9*

What I see happening to the image of business and capitalism in our country is not very good right now. The mainstream media works very hard to find fault with successful people. While saying they promote social justice, income equality, and fairness, they accomplish just the opposite by continually faulting the capitalist system as socially unjust, with unequal incomes and unfair business practices.

Judging Right from Wrong

I don't like to see our younger population questioning the very economic system that brought our country up from nothing to what we are today.

For many years, I was a judge at the Collegiate Business Ethics Contest. College teams had to sift through difficult decisions and make decisions on right and wrong business practices. You might think those decisions would be easy, but they weren't. We live in a very complicated world. Without the Golden Rule and biblical standards, I question whether they could do more than venture a guess on what was right.

At the Alpha Kappa Psi business fraternity's Principles of Leadership conventions, I judged and taught "Principles."

In my business involvement for over fifty years, I have seen many applications of both good and bad principles. I learned what worked and didn't work, and why. I helped businesses grow and become more profitable, returning greater rewards for me, our employees, and our shareholders.

146

The Bad and the Ugly

The huge size of a business should not, in itself, be proof that crimes are being committed. But when a few people at the top exercise so much control, the conditions are somewhat like a dictatorship. Generous leaders can direct a thriving organization, but greedy leaders can create an empire that will collapse when its injustices are discovered.

Public opinion of business declined substantially with the Enron and Health South scandals. Then Bernie Madoff and his gigantic scam came into the picture. Attitudes didn't improve with the unsurpassed greed of the big financial companies like Goldman Sachs, Lehman Brothers, and JP Morgan. What about the role of the politicians and CEOs that led to the financial instability of Fannie Mae and Freddy Mac? While our economy neared collapse, trillions of investment dollars were lost, and millions of jobs were lost—some city slickers made billions.

The bailout of General Motors and Chrysler gave unions an even better deal. Friends of the political system made millions. Lawyers and accountants made fortunes in one of the most blatant examples of crony capitalism of all time.

When we're sure the causes for failure aren't repeatable and the funds are a loan to provide a clear path to success, a bailout makes good sense. But when cronies get rich at the expense of the taxpayer, we've gone from bad to ugly.

Our government does so much of this on a grand scale, making up new rules as it goes along, I wonder how many other businesses will think these greedy practices are okay.

Outlandish Executive Salaries

If you want to see the most ridiculously high executive salaries, Google "pharmaceutical executive salaries." Maybe it doesn't bother you to see salaries higher than the best NFL quarterbacks, but what I see is a factor in why prescription costs are so high.

Not only are there exorbitant salaries, but bonuses, expense accounts, lavish severance pay, and other benefits add many millions to those numbers. My CEO salaries were nothing compared to what is paid today. I have to wonder if those huge salaries are in proportion to the value of their contribution to their companies. When the company is struggling financially, I have to say, definitely not.

How did we get to such extreme values? I think it has much to do with Wall Street greed—wanting to push stock prices higher. A company's board of directors is caught in the frenzy of offering unbelievably lucrative multi-year contracts in order to hire the most reputable person available. Board members want to keep their jobs, and they don't want to be sued for making bad decisions. This might be good and to be expected, but ridiculous payouts show greed and stupidity.

The Short-Selling Business

The lowest of scumbag business is the short-selling of stocks. An investor borrows shares and immediately sells them, hoping to scoop them up later at a lower price, return them to the lender, and pocket the difference.

The big money is made by manipulating a company's stock prices and use computer buys at the highest prices. Then they use a variety of ways to push the prices down. Blogging, social media, and Internet publications spin an array of bad news, which might have an element of truth but is grossly exaggerated. Some good companies have been ruined from these people's greed. They don't care about principles or have a value compass.

In the old days, we could hang horse thieves. Now, we've legalized thievery in the markets.

The Fall of Enron

I was once co-chair for a big event at our university. We booked Ken Lay, a past university graduate and CEO of Enron to be our guest speaker. He gave a passionate speech about the company's greatness, obviously believing everything he said. A few months later, Enron collapsed with its $40 billion in market value down the drain. The president and financial officers of Enron went off to jail. Ken Lay died of a heart attack just before his trial, falling from the pinnacle of success to perhaps the biggest business villain other than Bernie Madoff.

I think Ken Lay and the "smartest men in the room," as they were called, were following the advice of some high-powered lawyers, accountants, political friends, and government agencies—all of them approving the manipulations with shell companies and creative accounting. Their boards of directors were cheerleaders, supposedly getting rich on the escalating stock values. Rules and regulations were bent and reshaped to create the numbers needed for the market. What they didn't do was to ask themselves if their manipulations were ethical or right. The needle on their new-fashioned value compass got stuck in the wrong direction, and all the king's horses and men couldn't put the egg back together.

Pleasing Wall Street

Corporate action based on stock values raises a very big value question. As a CEO, I sometimes fantasized about some creative financing that I thought might help the company, but the idea went no further. My CFO said, "Yeah, we could do that." Then a long pause. "But we would probably end up in jail."

Ken Lay's president and CFO pleased his board of directors and those Enron stockholders. But when pleasing Wall Street crosses the line into the unethical and dishonest practices, they may be looking through prison bars, wondering where their prosperity went.

Simply following the old-fashioned Golden Rule would save a lot of grief.

Not So Smart

At a company where I was president, a principal shareholder was extremely successful, praised for being so smart. He treated me with kindness, and I thought he followed good principles. However, he was always consulting lawyers and consultants, walking close to the edge for personal gain.

In one scheme, he made a questionable stock transaction that bet against the success of our company, thinking it would return millions in personal profit. Technically, it was legal, but it smelled unethical. A *New York Times* editorial called him the "worst robber baron since the turn of the century." I think, when a deal smells bad, it probably is. Our stock values plummeted.

Later, with plenty of legal advice, he found schemes to avoid taxes, which the IRS and Justice Department said was illegal. The Feds stepped in, big time, to collect back taxes, forcing him into bankruptcy.

In court, he claimed to have done nothing wrong. He had only acted upon the best legal and accounting advice that money could buy. But the bankruptcy judge said, "You should have known better."

As he walked the unethical road that has become so popular in modern times, he became too smart for his own good. I think he abandoned old-fashioned values for the new approach that said anything was okay as long as expert advisors said so.

My grandmother would say, "He just got too big for his britches."

I think they had difficulty separating values and principles from their temptations. As Proverbs 16:18 says, "Pride goes before destruction, a haughty spirit before a fall."

Fundamental Principles

In what I called my "retirement years," I was brought in to three companies that were headed in the wrong direction, probably destined for bankruptcy. People sometimes ask if I recognized any common factors in their problems. Yes, there were several, all connected with fundamental principles that weren't followed.

First, when the board of directors and CEO become too greedy, they either don't want to understand or are simply ignorant of the complicated parts of the business. Directors brought in for diversity instead of valuable experience in the business can be a giant problem.

Second, taking on exorbitant debt to expand and help the company meet Wall Street expectations can be fatal. Board members and officers are tempted to ignore fundamental operational principles so they can have their big bonuses and increased stock values.

Third, cronyism and favoritism in the organization can dramatically encourage inadequate abilities, dysfunctional relationships, and bad performance. Values get clouded when this exists.

Most of the time, greed, not external problems, were the root cause for thee big problems that eventually led to bankruptcy. Principles in leadership disappeared along the way. Their value compass didn't work.

What Works

Is capitalism good? Absolutely. It has made our country as wonderful as it is today.

But for capitalism to work, we must have ambition, desire, a reasonable amount of ability, and follow the biblical principles of love, kindness, and service.

Temptation to be greedy and unethical for personal benefit is always nearby. We don't have to look far to find "loop holes" for bending the rules for integrity and still be "legal." If our priority is what we can get for ourselves, and we're not that concerned for helping others, we're most likely headed for trouble.

Old-fashioned honesty is being tested like never before. Modern values tend to expect lying and cheating as normal, and rules, regulations, and tax codes have become so complicated, we're encouraged to milk the system for all it's worth.

High-powered lawyers, accountants, and leaders on Wall Street may tell us that pushing the envelope is a wonderful thing, but when it takes us away from our old-fashioned values so we care only for ourselves and not for others, bankruptcy could be right around the corner.

What Lies Ahead

The future of our country must be built on the strong foundation of trust. There was a time when biblical principles stood strong, and we labeled our currencies with the message: *In God We Trust*. If people did more of that, behaviors would improve, and we'd see more trust in one another.

I'm seeing cracks in our foundation of trust, because the love of money is promoting distrust, the root of all evil. If our values continue in that direction, capitalism cannot succeed, and socialism will be worse.

New-fashioned political correctness is not the way to a better society. Biblical principles centered on loving God and caring for our neighbors—even strangers and enemies—show us the best way to live, the best way to do business.

If we can to return to our old-fashioned values, our future can be very bright.

Drugs to Cure or Kill

*Physical training is of some value, but godliness has value
for all things, holding promise for both the present life
and the life to come. — 1 Timothy 4:8*

In the last fifty years, advertising has made the public more and
more aware of their need for drugs to solve their physical and
emotional problems.

Quick, Easy Cure

If we have a pain, a discomfort somewhere, there must be a pill for
it. Years ago, the common approach was to take two aspirin. If we
didn't feel better in the morning, then call the doctor. Now, we
want something much stronger than aspirin.

In this country, drug companies can advertise their products to
the public. On television ads, we hear pleasant background music
and see smiling people enjoying the drug's benefits. At the end
we're given a quick list of possible side-effects, as if those probably
wouldn't apply to us. We should contact our doctor.

If I just pay attention to the words, ignoring the video and audio,
the advertisement offers a drug that *might* help one of our ailments.
On the other hand, we *might* get worse in not just one but maybe a
dozen different ways. But that's not the way the ad is typically
perceived. Apparently, this drug must be a quick, easy cure.

A Drugged Nation

The pharmaceutical companies' values need an overhaul.
Prescription drug use per person is by far the highest in our
country, and I believe that use has quadrupled in the last twenty

years. How else could we solve all the problems with PTSD, ADD, ADHD, panic, and depression?

To feel better, we've turned to alcohol, nicotine, and prescription drugs, but that hasn't been enough. We now have a growing desire to legalize drugs whose sale and use have sent people to jail.

High Prices

The cost of "miracle" drugs can be astronomical, running into the thousands of dollars per month. With great insurance, just the copay can be more than we can afford. But we must pay it. We're told we have no choice.

If the public knew how many of our tax dollars subsidize the big drug companies and knew how much politicians gain from supporting these companies, we would recognize the greed and a problem with people's values. But we'll never see those number advertised.

In 1950, a pack of cigarettes cost 25 cents. Twenty years later, the cost was about a nickel more. But now, after we've added taxes and government regulation, people will pay $5, and in some states, more than twice that. We have some companies, politicians, and governments that are collecting lots of dollars because of our addictions.

The Good Old Days

I long for the old days when a doctor told us what we really needed to treat our ailments. We never thought we were supposed to tell the doctor what medicine to prescribe. Growing up, I was told to "not practice medicine without a license." Modern advertising and our addictions have changed those values.

In the old days, print advertising could be open and honest about the facts, because we didn't have all the fancy drugs with their side-effects. Since the law requires their listing, we see them in such small type that they can't be read without a magnifying glass.

154

Money for Research

The defense for all of this nebulous drug advertising says, "The extra marketing is necessary to fund research." Sounds great, but is it true? Where do those dollars actually go? Tens of millions of dollars support politicians. Some might argue that this leads to legislation to fund research, but that's done with our tax dollars, not campaign funds.

In looking over the expenditures for some of the large companies, I found that the industry was spending billions of dollars for advertising. Almost twice as much was for marketing than for research and development. Obviously, they are more interested in growing their market and making money, and not so much for research and development that would improve benefits and at lower cost.

In looking at the political contributions, I'm thinking I might need a pill for my depression. In one year, pharmaceutical companies spent almost $200 million lobbying the federal government, which was more than any other industry. The amount of the contributions keeps going up. Companies do that to make money, not as a patriotic duty to support our country. I can't help but wonder what kind of return on investment they are getting.

Bad Drugs

I believe Levaquin, a drug manufactured by Ortho-McNeil Pharmaceutical, a subsidiary of Johnson & Johnson, almost killed me. After taking this drug, I suffered terrible side-effects. My lungs ruptured, and I was spitting up blood by the quart. The long story about this was published in Roaring Lambs' *Stories of Roaring Faith Volume 2.*

Given less than a day to live, I was flown to the Mayo Clinic in Rochester, Minnesota, where I was diagnosed with Wegener's Disease. Something had caused my B cells to attack my lungs. They wouldn't say for sure that Levaquin was responsible, but I'm convinced. After ten years, I've still not fully recovered.

This drug is still prescribed, but we should be concerned about any drug's possible side effects. Maybe it helped others, but the side-effects, like any allergic reaction, could kill you.

Good Drugs

No matter the cause, my very rare Wegener's Disease required treatment. A nurse discovered an experimental drug that just might work. Doctors from some of the country's leading institutions were conducting a survey, and I got to be number 53 in that survey, which was *not* conducted by the drug company. Several years later, the drug was approved by the FDA for prescription use.

Since I am now in remission, I have reason to be personally thankful for all the research and development costs that have brought good drugs to market. The not-so-good part is what they cost. When I read about the same drug in Canada costing half as much, I have to ask if all the advertising, political contributions, and lobbying expense is good.

Corporate Greed

Most people think businesses make 30 to 40 percent profit, but that's nowhere close to true. Walmart makes a little over 2 percent, and the average for all companies is around 8 percent. Even the big oil companies do well to clear 6 percent. So the idea that private enterprise is taking advantage of consumers, taking excessive profits, just isn't the case for most sectors. The drug companies are a different matter.

When companies like Eli Lilly, Schering-Plough, and Bristol Myers show 25 to 30 percent profit on revenue, you're looking at some businesses that exceed what we normally see in free enterprise. Typically, what makes enterprise less free is government control and a lack of competition. With the pharmaceutical companies, we have both, which explains how this industry could be approaching a trillion dollars in profits over the next decade.

Price Manipulation

When a company owns the patent on a drug and no generic substitute exists, they are free to push prices up as high as their exclusive marked will bear. I've seen a $57 drug skyrocket to $600. That change wasn't because of the high cost of production. It was to make a lot of money for chief executives, stock holders, and politicians.

156

I once read about a provision the pharmaceutical lobby inserted into the law to prohibit Medicare or Medicaid from using its unparalleled purchasing power to obtain discounts or negotiate prices with drug companies. By prohibiting Medicare to get better drug prices, the federal government was effectively subsidizing the greed of the drug makers and their CEOs.

I am not complaining about profits. Without them, companies couldn't stay in business. A lot of my IRA is invested in drug companies. My biggest single holding is a healthcare mutual fund. What I'm complaining about is too much profit that makes just a few people rich while making many seniors struggle to pay for their prescriptions.

Drug Epidemic

The pill-pushing doctors, influenced by pill-pushing drug companies, have promoted monumental addictions to prescription drugs, especially opioids. Our government has spent hundreds of millions of dollars in the war on drugs, but from what I can see, people are more addicted now than before.

Principles in Journalism

Dear friends, do not believe every spirit, but test the spirits to see whether they are from God, because many false prophets have gone out into the world. — 1 John 4:1

I am not sure what has happened to journalism. It certainly isn't what it used to be, when reporters were expected to tell the truth, the whole truth, and nothing but the truth.

Old-Fashioned Rules

When I attended journalism classes, I was taught *principles*. Supposedly, ethical journalism strives for free exchange of information that is accurate, fair, and thorough. If I wanted a good grade, I had to follow the rules. If I had wanted to flunk, I would have plagiarized, distorted people's words, and presented narrow opinions as if they were fact—like many so-called journalists do today.

I was taught principles of integrity, with a clear separation of news from the editorial pages of opinions. Personal bias and favoring a political view had no place in news articles. We were to seek the truth, reporting only the facts as they could be substantiated. Back then, journalism was a respected profession.

Opinions were encouraged, but they had to be labeled as such, not passed off as news. Truth in advertising was crucial. If a claim couldn't be substantiated or was misleading in some way, regulatory agencies or the media itself would demand corrections and apologies.

In my old-fashioned days, people who didn't follow the rules stood out like ketchup on a white suit. They were always exposed.

Tsunami of New Rules

In many ways, the old rules have been swept out to sea and replaced with opposite values. Where bad conduct was once condemned, it can now be justified if not glamorized. Conservative dress and professional appearance in advertising has been replaced by scanty dress, partial nudity, and sexually suggestive poses. Language that was once reserved for crusty old sailors is now a part of everyday speech.

My grandma would have been shocked if she could see the Super Bowl halftime show or the American Music Awards. She didn't know media from cake mix, but she wouldn't miss the difference between proper behavior and lewd appearance and speech.

Nothing could be better than what we see on television screens and the Internet to reveal society's completely revised set of rules.

Polarized Glasses

Turn on network television today, and you'll see news slanted toward whatever color the newscasters are seeing through, either red or blue. They may call themselves journalists, but they are mainly a bunch of actors with just the right appearance and voice to express the bias of conservative or liberal writers, catering to an equally polarized audience.

Blogs can be written by anyone who wants to cater to special interests and gather an audience sympathetic to a particular point of view. No journalistic qualifications or experience is required. Supposed "facts" don't have to be substantiated. The blogger only needs to cater to what the audience wants to believe.

What bothers me the most is the pay that many of these actors get for acting like journalists. We seem to be offering entertainment more than education. The polls I've read indicate that the trust of television news reporting is about the same as our respect for lawyers, congress, and used-car salesmen—only slightly above horse thieves.

Yellow Journalism

Way back when, sensational journalism, focused on popularity rather than principle, was called "yellow journalism," a symbol for fancy dress designed to attract a huge audience. I'm not sure how to describe the styles used today. In all my years, I have never seen such bias and sensationalism in journalism. The teasers and fanfare can get more emphasis than the actual reports.

The progressive media seems determined to change our country to their views, their values, their principles, while demonizing opposing points of view.

Newspapers

Printed newspapers seem to be losing their importance, like typewriters and wooden buckets. I must be old-fashioned, because I still read my local newspaper for an hour each morning while having coffee.

I'd like to say that what I read brightens my day, but sometimes I get so disgusted with violations of old-fashioned journalism principles that I feel like a teapot ready to spew steam.

I read several columns that should have been moved to the editorial section as opinion pieces. I didn't think they belonged with factual reporting, not since they argued in favor of people's "constitutional right" to burn the American flag. The writing was unfair, biased, politically prejudiced propaganda that our old-fashioned values would have rejected, saying those arguments belonged in a communist paper. The articles didn't motivate me to burn the flag. But I did want to go out and burn the newspaper.

There was a day long ago when *The New York Times* was a wonderful paper. I didn't mind the biased editorial section, because writers gave a pretty straight shot at publishing the news. Not anymore. Now we see much of their news slanted to suit their political perspective. This has become so important that some reporters have been caught fabricating stories to make a political point, yet they were defended by the paper and weren't fired.

I believe it was Mark Twain who said you're uninformed if you don't read the paper, but if you do read it, you're misinformed. If he saw that happening back then, he would be shocked to read a newspaper today.

Political Agenda

I've read reports that say 96 percent of reporters favor one political party. They sit on one side of the aisle, pointing out all the bad people on the other side. And no matter what the other side is doing, the action is always labeled as bad.

I wonder if people will ever take a step back, look objectively at the situation, and determine the truth. Or will we keep cheering whatever bias matches what we want to believe?

If we could focus on old-fashioned values that sought the truth, we might be able to solve problems rather than make them bigger with our words.

Moral Decline

I don't know whether modern television programming is a result or a cause for moral decline. Maybe each one supports the other in a gradual, persistent move away from biblical values. The Ten Commandments first became ten *suggestions*, which are now becoming old-fashioned rules to be ignored.

Entertainment has become more important than education. Getting is valued above giving. We follow the fool's golden rule that wants to file suit whenever we've been mistreated. We live for the pursuit of pleasure, caring mostly about ourselves, very little about the needs of anyone else. The end justifies the means, so lying, cheating, and stealing becomes acceptable as long as we have a good reason and don't get caught.

Movies and television glorify violence, promiscuous sex, and drug use. Where have our moral principles gone?

Imaginary Truth

I believe many of our old-fashioned values have been taken over by the educated elite who don't believe in God and think we can decide the truth, whether something is right or wrong. Since they are so smart, others are obviously deplorable dummies for not believing as they do. Seeing their motives as pure, they have erected

161

utopias in their minds—constructing a false reality that allows them to feel good about themselves, their beliefs, and their practices. They use "social justice" to manipulate the minds of young people to rely on the government for their success instead of trusting God and serving people.

Journalism has changed a lot. Apparently, that is what many Americans want—imaginary truth instead of the real truth.

I hope my fellow Americans will stand strong, check their value compasses, and demand old-fashioned principles in journalism's value system.

Education Today

Not many of you should become teachers,
my fellow believers, because you know that we who teach
will be judged more strictly. — *James 3:1*

I get confused with what is going on in public education. What happened to old Reading, wRiting and aRithmetic that we knew as the three Rs? Those used to be important values.

Test Results

Values seem to have changed for the worst, because test results show the knowledge of those three basic skills are lower than they used to be. The value of the three Rs may be in serious trouble.

As the government has become more involved and more money is being poured into public education, the scores haven't been getting better. The bullying and violence in schools have definitely gotten worse.

We could blame the problem on the ills of our society. For forty years, I've been hearing that we need to spend more money on education. We keep saying we need to do more, because the "more" we've been doing each year hasn't been enough.

Collective Bargaining

In some states, teachers unions have been downright violent. What are they demanding? They say, "Your kids' futures are at stake," which is misleading if they're picketing for higher pay and more benefits. I don't see where better retirement and more on their paychecks is going to improve the curriculum and teaching methods.

As the test scores keep going down while the dropout rate and costs go up, collective bargaining seems to be more about helping the union and its members, not so much for the kids.

Spending More

I read that our country poured $2 trillion into improving public schools in the last few years. I wonder what those tax dollars paid for. Cleaner, more modern buildings, perhaps. Better security. Support for sports, band, and the arts? All that may be good and necessary, but I'm wondering how much actually went for Reading, wRiting and aRithmetic.

I saw a recent picture of the small-town school I attended. I counted four times as many teachers, coaches, counselors, and assistants than when I was there with a lot more students. I don't understand why we need more people to accomplish less.

I wonder what would happen if we spent as much on academics as we spend on building and maintaining football stadiums. My old-fashioned values say we should take a serious look at our ROI—Return on Investment. How much value did we get for the tax dollars paid out?

New Standards

In my schooldays, I don't think anyone in my little community ever felt deprived, although we lived below poverty level by today's standards. Somehow we survived without air conditioning and lunch programs. We did pretty well with one teacher for thirty students, no counselors, and one coach for athletics.

Parents provided breakfast at home and made sure we had a sack lunch for school. None of the kids were overfed and fat. We were slim and trim. We walked. We played. We worked.

We didn't know about the new standards, or we would have felt deprived. Instead, we studied hard and learned a lot.

Graduating Ignorance

Most graduating high school seniors have trouble naming the first three American presidents. I'm guessing they got that right on their history test, but that information is now forgotten because it was never really learned. Some seniors would have to guess who Lewis and Clark were. Perhaps a rock band. Do they know anything about the Korean War? Have they heard of the Gettysburg Address? Probably not. Maybe it's a street near Pennsylvania Avenue.

Old-fashioned penmanship is now a lost art. If cursive writing is taught at all, it isn't emphasized. I wonder how far we are from having to make our "mark," because we don't know how to sign our name.

I've read that geography test scores are lower now than they were ten years ago. On military entrance exams, many young men can't answer simple questions like "If $2 + X = 4$, what is the value of X." After high school graduation, people should be able to figure out what to add to 2 to get 4.

Something is wrong with our value system when we parade students across the stage and hand them a diploma when they've not learned the three Rs.

Minority Education

I've read that minorities tend to score much lower on the ACT tests that measure college readiness in English, math, reading, and science. I'm sure there are exceptions on both sides, but I wonder why this is true, generally speaking. Unless we're brain damaged, we're all capable.

The differences in culture might lead to challenges in communication between teachers and students. Environmental differences, especially dysfunctional parenting situations, might be a significant distraction from learning. I've read many cases where disadvantaged minorities overcame huge obstacles in education and became very successful. That tells me that the opportunities are there for all kids to do well—if they want to.

If a *desire* to learn is most crucial, then I fear we may be trying to fix the wrong thing by adding teachers or medicating students. Maybe we need some old-fashioned values that excite people about learning and quit saying the government should make life easier.

Money or Message

I am all for spending more for education if we can get a reasonable return for that investment. We might also find that cutbacks in some non-academic areas would shift focus where it matters most. I know that many young football players dream of playing in the NFL, but more than 99 percent won't make it. Even the small percentage who get a pro contract will only last a few years and will then be like the 99 percent, needing a good education to succeed in the business world.

I'm amazed at how well private Christian schools educate their students, and they do it at less than half the cost of public education. What do they do differently that might be a factor in their success?

For one, parents pay significant tuition costs, which is in addition to their taxes that go to support public education. That out-of-pocket expense gives parents a vested interest in what their children are learning. No longer is education assumed to be "free," so they are more likely to be sure their children pay attention in class and do their homework.

Since public education pays much higher salaries, teachers in private Christian schools must have a reason for working for less money. Most likely, they care more about what they are teaching and how well their students are learning. And if the teachers care more, that attitude can be contagious among students.

In a Christian school, attendance at chapel is mandatory. The Golden Rule and honorable behavior is weaved into all that is said and done. The atmosphere is more about encouragement, not intimidation, never ridicule.

When a problem arises with a student, communication between everyone concerned will be much better, simply because it has to be based on Christian principles. Without a doubt, the message matters more than the money, because when the message is wrong, no amount of money will fix the problem.

Old-fashioned values matter, because the new-fashioned values are severely lacking in biblically based principles. If we could have more of that at home and at school, all forms of education would be better.

Special Programs

Today we have all kinds of special education programs, which we obviously think are important. We have enhancement programs, social programs, bullying programs, fear programs, and whatever new message we might contrive for political correctness. The government and the department of education force-feed a lot of this stuff. Some schools won't graduate a student without a passing knowledge of "protecting the environment." I wonder if it's more important to make convincing arguments about climate change than to teach the three Rs.

We have ethnic culture courses for minorities, which emphasize racial disadvantages and abuses by police. Our country is described as a mean place, which encourages violence and protests. This may not be the intent, but minority student behaviors suggest that something isn't right about the messages.

Obsolete Programs

I wonder what happened to the old-fashioned work/school apprentice programs that trained students for a vocation. Do we still have shop classes? Are we training young men for auto mechanics? We have a lot of graduating seniors who don't know how to use a wrench, screwdriver, or radial saw. Most haven't changed a flat tire or replaced a burned-out headlight.

Do we still teach Home Economics? If so, I doubt that many young women are taking the course. Many have no desire to clean house or cook. Restaurants need good chefs and servers. Where is the training for that?

Discipline

In the old days, the "board of education" was what you felt strike your bottom for not standing in line or for talking too much. Anyone caught in a fight might be too sore to sit down for a while. I don't know what would have happened if someone mouthed off at a teacher, because that behavior was unthinkable. After seeing an out-of-line student get licks, nobody considered doing anything worse.

Now, a teacher can be fired for grabbing a misbehaving student by the shoulder or saying something that might be offensive. The old saying, "Spare the rod, spoil the child," has been replaced with "Talk nice and don't touch, or the child will hurt you."

I wonder if we've watered down discipline so much that rebellious students have little respect for authority and little interest in education.

Private Schools

If we can't get government out of the schools, maybe we should get the schools out of government, taking them private, free from all the political mandates. In the last fifty years, we've developed new values that prevent public schools having any form of allegiance to God or country. But if private schools don't depend on government funds, they can still have the Lord's Prayer and the Pledge of Allegiance every day.

My wife and I sent our first two children to public schools, but after seeing the quality of education deteriorate, we sent our youngest daughter to private school. We're now helping pay for our grandchildren to attend private schools. We still pay taxes that support public schools. We think the additional cost for them to attend private schools instead of public schools is an excellent investment. All our grandchildren are doing are doing very well in school.

Many parents want their children to have a better education, but they can't afford private schools. They want vouchers that would let them recoup some of their tax dollars, which would help them pay for private schooling. Of course, teachers unions and lobbyists will fight that all the way to the Supreme Court if necessary.

No Child Left Behind

Almost twenty years ago, Congress passed legislation that was supposed to help all the students who were lagging behind. By assessing basic skills and attaining minimum standards for federal funding, legislators expected the quality of education to improve. I don't think that program has met its goals. I see students taught to make better scores on tests, but not how to think for themselves and learn more. They remain pretty much unprepared for the business world after graduation.

Maybe some kids should be left behind if they are not willing to *work* at getting an education. Many are dropping out before graduation. When that happens, the schools lose revenue, so we might expect districts to do all they can to keep students and promote them with overly generous grading. That's the new-fashioned way to leave no child behind.

I like the old-fashioned values better. If students can't make the grade, they should be allowed to fail. Virtually all students who are willing to pay attention in class and do homework will have passing grades, and just that change would move many from the barely passing level to excellence.

Not the Teacher's Fault

I know there are a few bad teachers around. That's true for every profession, including law enforcement and church ministries. But if we consider what these people must tolerate in dealing with difficult people, sometimes on a daily basis, we should recognize some degree of self-sacrifice in the interest of helping others.

I love teachers. My wife has a degree in education and taught in public schools for many years, working long hours for some outstanding results. After more than a decade of teaching, she left the profession. Why? No one seemed to care if she produced great results or not. She got the same pay raises as those who did little more than show up for work.

When progressive school administrators want to make improvements, they are usually fighting a losing battle against teachers unions, community organizers, and politicians. Many old-fashioned values have a proven track record. We know they will work again, but once rejected, they are next to impossible to re-introduce into our political, government-run systems.

Academic Capitalism

If you call out for insight and cry aloud for understanding
... as for silver and ... hidden treasure, then
you will understand the fear of the Lord and find
the knowledge of God. — *Proverbs 2:3–5*

I know that many politicians love socialism and hate capitalism, but there's a reason why capitalism works and socialism doesn't. If we could replace a won't-work socialism value with a will-work capitalism value, we would add a positive while subtracting a negative. I don't know how good you are with math, but that adds up to a double-positive.

Return on Investment.

ROI is a business term that measures benefits gained from time, effort, and money spent. Will a million dollars in advertising produce $100 thousand additional sales and $10 thousand profit? That's probably not a good deal. Better cut the advertising budget or come up with something more effective.

How might that capitalism principle apply to government-run education? The socialism values assume that if we spend more money on the problem, conditions have to get better. But history refuses to confirm that assumption. Socialism cares more about talking a good game rather than actually playing and checking the score. Capitalism simply wants to know if we've spent wisely, or if we might do something different to get more for less cost. This is what businesses must do constantly—or a successful business will soon be passed by a competitor and be forced out of business.

Healthy Competition

Since government agencies typically have no competition, managers don't have to worry about being competitive. Their incentive is to spend all their budget and present arguments that more funding is needed. This is the American socialism way: just hire more workers to compensate for inefficiency and low productivity. Capitalism insists on high performance. Employees who aren't doing a very good job are either fired or are transferred to responsibilities that better suit their abilities.

How could education be improved with competition? You're probably familiar with competition between schools for football, basketball, and track. But what about academics? We don't hear much about that. Texas has University Interscholastic League competition for a number of academic categories, including Accounting, Computer Applications, and Essays. At one time, we had Number Sense, Slide Rule, and Poetry Recitation, but those areas don't have the same value today. You probably wouldn't be surprised if I told you that academic competition gets less than a tenth as much attention as sports.

In an age where political correctness calls for giving every player a trophy, promoting the best teachers and replacing the worst would not be a popular move. Private enterprises have no choice but to do that if they want to stay in business. If we could apply just a few of those old-fashioned principles for teachers, the quality of education would have to improve.

Worldwide Rankings

Most Americans like to think of us as academically superior to other countries, but that's not where we are typically ranked among industrial nations. It isn't cheap labor that makes Germany rank so high. Their education system is different. Unlike our country, Germany doesn't preach equality among all students, that everyone should attend college and achieve management status for the most high-paying jobs. After the basics are taught in the lower grades, some go to universities, but many go to trade schools to learn valuable skills in plumbing, electrical, mechanics, and engineering.

Instead of trying to fit all students to the curriculum, they are fitting different curriculums to the different ways people act and think.

In the home construction industry, most workers are Hispanic and speak little English. Gringos might become managers if they had the opportunity to learn construction from the ground up. And for today's market, they would have to be fluent in Spanish. Since our socialite education system doesn't support that, most managers are Hispanic, fluent in both Spanish and English.

If we applied some capitalism values in educating for the trades, we could rank our academic minds with similar groups in other companies and rise from twenty-fifth in math, reading, and science to near the top.

Who ranks very high? The Chinese in Hong Kong, Singapore, and mainland China. Americans rank low because our university students are of a different grouping from theirs. The Chinese universities accept only the best academic minds in which an A+ grade is excellent and an A- grade is close to failing. American university students don't have the same interests, because so many are more focused on sports, dating, and parties.

Copycats

The Chinese understand ROI really well. They may be communists but they act like capitalists in the way they run their education opportunities. They definitely believe in competition.

The Chinese have no shame in copying things invented by others. Mainland China seems to have copied Singapore's educational system. Obviously, they are not copying our system. What fool wouldn't want to copy the best? America, perhaps, since I'm seeing politicians argue in favor of socialism that has failed in other countries. As smart as we can be, sometimes we can act really foolish.

The Chinese have made education a privilege that students and teachers value and compete for. Their system demands hard work and rewards performance. That sounds a lot like capitalism in which winners get the prize. Not everybody gets a trophy.

Our public school system pays teachers based on years of experience and degrees held. Unions and education associations fight aggressively against making teachers accountable for student

172

achievement. They claim that a merit system degrades already low employee morale by pitting teachers against their peers. It's back to that new-fashioned idea that everybody deserves a trophy. Having winners and losers is an old-fashioned capitalism idea that should be shunned. They say competition among students is harmful, because only the winner feels good and everybody else is a loser. People may think I'm old and outdated, but I'm still young enough to remember the principles of capitalism that worked in education as well as business. We should copy some of that, and not the socialism practices that haven't work for other countries and will never work for us.

Laziness

In China, lazy and indifferent students, who do not value an education, are not tolerated. We think all students are created equal, but they recognize all students as *not* equal. In capitalism, American businesses know how true this is, but socialism rules may require them to hire a less-capable applicant who fits the required racial or ethnic profile. Chinese students have an incentive to get off their butts and work at getting an education.

By recognizing the need to steer some students to productive trades instead of universities, China is basically identifying the square pegs for square holes, the round pegs for round holes. The American way tries to make everyone conform to the same shape. The hopelessness and frustration of the American way is an educational incentive killer, promoting laziness, while the Chinese students are energized by knowing their abilities fit what they are expected to accomplish.

I am not saying China has all of the answers. Their communist government has countless problems, but that shouldn't keep us from recognizing what they do well, particularly in the educational area where they apply old-fashioned capitalism principles and demand a return on investment.

The Bad Mistake

In Dallas, we set up high school graduates to fail by ignoring vocation and technical colleges. About six out of ten graduates will apply for college, but two won't show up. Of the remaining four, at least three won't earn a degree. Their higher-level education won't get them a better job, but it will put them at least $25 thousand in debt with no ability to pay.

With more than a trillion dollars in college tuition debt, much of which will never be paid, we can be sure the return on investment of our tax dollars is horrendous. We are going in the wrong direction by not emphasizing trade and skill training. Maybe we're doing well at the start, in the lower grades, but our system isn't helping many students finish the race.

Catholic Schools

I think one reason Catholic school education has an edge is the capitalism approach to people for their unique abilities and value, with self-discipline required of each individual. That expectation applies both to teachers and students. Areas with heavy black and Hispanic enrollment show higher achievement, better graduation rates, and more college enrollments than nearby public schools.

Also, we should never underestimate the power of biblical principles in education. While that's been lost in public schools, it remains part of the Catholic educational process. Without a doubt, the God-fearing atmosphere of that environment has a positive effect, not just on a child's behavior but also how well they learn. When my grandchildren went to Catholic schools, I could see where I was getting a very high return on my investment.

Waking Up

I doubt whether my fellow Americans will wake up and demand a refund for all their tax money wasted on ineffective public education. But looking forward, we might want to raise our voice for academic capitalism that demands a return on our investment. If we do that, we could again become a leader in the world market, both in education and in commerce.

If we don't speak up, saying old-fashioned values matter, then they won't matter.

Being Presidential

Remember your leaders, who spoke the word of God
to you. Consider the outcome of their way of life
and imitate their faith. — Hebrews 13:7

The ancient Jews had both righteous and evil kings, and this country has had both good, God-fearing leaders and those who were not so good. Many people today aren't aware of what our founding fathers did for us, giving us a Constitution based on Judeo-Christian principles.

Lack of Knowledge

Whoever said, "Ignorance is bliss," must not have understood that what we don't know will catch us unaware and can lead to costly mistakes, even death. The Bible says people are destroyed for lack of knowledge (Hosea 4:6).

I'm sorry that we don't do a better job teaching American history. Not only do we not teach the value of our Christian heritage, but we want to tear down our statues that might cause us to remember our leaders' deeds, both good and bad. If we don't know what those conditions were, we are in danger of repeating the bad and not knowing to do the good.

Benefit of Age

As long as we don't suffer from Alzheimer's, getting older has the benefit of knowing more history first-hand. I am old enough to have lived under the administrations of thirteen presidents. Some have been better than others. Some stand at the top of my list, not because they never made mistakes but because I have seen them make significant contributions to the wellbeing of our country. But others many have hurt us more than they helped.

I watched as voters placed different men in our country's greatest leadership position, first during the World War II years with Franklin D. Roosevelt, Harry S. Truman, and Dwight D. Eisenhower. I remember the assassination of our thirty-fifth president, John F. Kennedy, and Vice President Lyndon Johnson taking the president's oath of office. The Watergate scandal and cover-up led to President Richard Nixon's resignation, with Gerald Ford taking his place. Jimmy Carter gave us wage and price controls that didn't work during the gasoline shortages. Ronald Reagan showed leadership skills far above what one might expect from a movie actor. He was followed by George H. W. Bush, Bill Clinton, and George W. Bush, then Barak Obama and finally, Donald Trump. They all had different values.

Respect for the Office

As soon as I was old enough, I voted for who I thought was the best candidate. My vote didn't always match the majority of electoral votes that elected our president, so I was naturally disappointed with the outcome. But I never thought to badmouth the president or openly attack him.

Whether we like the new president or not, for the good of our country we need to support him as best we can. In the old days, that's what we did. But our society's new-fashioned style wants to attack everything the political party in power does, even if it requires reversing past beliefs of the party no longer in power.

My old-fashioned values say I should respect the office of the president, even if I don't always like what he says or does. Now, we seem to be spending so much effort tearing others down that we can't build anything good.

Deplorable Support

In 2016, I was prepared to accept and support a president who had called me deplorable and despicable. Until then, I'd never been labeled as homophobic, Islamophobic, misogynist, racist, and sexist. Apparently, it takes one to know one, because I saw more of that kind of behavior among the accusers, not the accused.

I believed that candidate did not like me very much and didn't deserve my vote. Even so, if elected, I would have respected the office.

Popularity Contests

As November 2016 approached, many Americans believed the country had been going in the wrong direction. I remember Franklin Graham at a large rally in Austin saying we were in trouble spiritually, racially, and economically. I think we're in trouble politically as well.

Because of my old-fashioned biblical values and knowledge of why capitalism works and socialism doesn't, you might call me conservative, but that doesn't make me a Republican. I think we're in trouble on both sides of the political aisle. We're spending way too much time and effort making ourselves popular with voters. I wish the political constituencies demanded the truth and would only listen to realistic solutions, but that is not the case. Instead, we are too easily satisfied by charismatic appearances and empty promises that often avoid debates on the most crucial issues.

The future of this nation should not be in the hands of whoever wins the popularity contest. We're foolish to think partisan politics on either side will give us much hope. What we most need for our country is a lot of prayer, trusting God, and casting our votes for candidates who are most qualified for the office, not because they're popular and make us feel good.

The Lesser of Two Evils

In political campaigns, we hear so much badmouthing about the opposition and so little said about the real issues, we're not sure what to believe. We probably trust politicians less than lawyers and used-car salesmen. If they aren't lying, we at least expect them to twist the truth, so we're not 100 percent comfortable with any candidate. We're left with voting for whoever we think is the lesser of two evils.

In the old days, I was told anyone could become president. Now I believe it. They just have to be the most popular.

I wish the selection of party candidates was focused on qualifications, but it's more about political posturing and popularity than ability to do the job. Therefore, the primaries don't give us the most qualified candidate in the final election.

For this to change, I believe the people will have to demand it, returning to many of our old-fashioned, biblically based values.

Media Bias

Very few voters get close enough to candidates to know how they really feel and what they actually are capable of doing. They won't research a candidate's past voting records and public statements to see if their actions match their words. Most people form their opinions about candidates from what they watch on television and what family and friends say.

Viewers who watch the mainstream media are given a positive outlook on candidates with more liberal, socialistic values. Those who pay attention to conservative newscasts and talk shows get a positive outlook on candidates who value capitalism and biblical principles. Most viewers will watch only the broadcasts that cater to what they want to believe.

If we don't know a candidate personally, we need to understand that all we know is what we've been told. And if we're only seeing the conservative or liberal views, we may be allowing ourselves to be politically biased without knowing we've been brainwashed.

Crooked Politics

I believe it was President Harry S. Truman who said you can't get rich in politics unless you're a crook. If he was thinking that back in the 1940s, how much worse might those conditions be now? I'm looking at all the candidates who got rich after they were elected and wonder what crooked dealings are going on. If the media knows but isn't telling us, then they are complicit in the crimes.

Sometimes I wonder if some of these people might be in the group that claimed to have done many wonderful works, but in the last days, Jesus condemns them (Matthew 7:22–23). At the end, what will label their apparently good works as bad? Perhaps it's using their power and position to make themselves rich instead of doing very much to help the people.

Stuck on Values

President Truman was known for the sign on his desk that said, *The BUCK STOPS here!* He was always one to stick with his values and make no excuses. He would listen to advisors, but then he would make what he believed was the right decision—like the total destruction of Hiroshima and Nagasaki in Japan. Because of his order, many innocent lives were lost, but it immediately ended the war and saved countless American lives.

In modern times, what we call war is more about political posturing to please the American electorate than it is to fight for freedom and do what's right. We know that's true when we'll sacrifice our American soldiers' lives to avoid being condemned for taking one innocent life. I don't like war, but if it's necessary to protect our freedoms and keep us safe, our soldiers shouldn't be marched to the battlefront but not be allowed to fire on the enemy without first getting permission from a president and political leaders who don't understand war.

The Great Divide

How did we ever get so divided in our values? If we're looking for answers, we should follow the money trail. The media deserves an awful lot of credit for the division. Why? The more controversy they can stir up, the better their ratings and the more money they make.

To survive, every radio or television show must remain popular with viewers. Fair and balanced reporting of the issues doesn't do much to stir emotion in the audience. Since a biased approach has better potential for making money, broadcasts tend to be very one-sided in one political direction or the other, even to the point of absurdity. Almost all news reporters love one candidate while hating the opponent, so they expand the positive coverage for the candidate they like and focus on every negative they can find for the candidate they don't like. This used to be true during the campaigns but calmed after the elections. Not anymore.

After the election, opponents continue to attack the president and his party's leaders. Why? For one thing, ratings are helped by keeping the audience stirred up. But besides that, another congressional election comes in just two years and the presidential election comes in four. In the old days, two or four years seemed like a long time, but now, politicians are campaigning for the next election just as soon as the last event is over.

The problem with this warfare is a lack of true winners. Obviously, the losers didn't win. But the winners are now being attacked more fiercely. With the war still raging, with no peace in sight, they haven't really won.

Choosing Sides

Straddling the fence is not a comfortable way to walk. Two opposing views cannot both be right. Either we value biblical principles and the capitalism values or we want to distance ourselves from God and endorse socialism. Strong Christians may have issues with the Republican point of view, but they'll struggle even more with the anti-God, free sex, and pro-choice views of the Democrat platform.

An abyss separates the two sides, but the liberal socialism side seems to be throwing the most rocks. Past presidents George H. W. Bush and George W. Bush were silent after an opposing president was elected, refusing to stir controversy from the Republican side. On the other hand, Hillary Clinton spent years campaigning bitterly about her loss and describing how horrible the new president was. Past president Obama has been much more outspoken about his dislike for the new president, even when that means arguing against the policies he supported while in office.

Before you choose which side to take, I want you to consider what matters most—our old-fashioned values that once served us well. Support the candidates who stand for truth and biblical values, and never miss a chance to vote. If more of us would do that, the two sides might have to agree on something.

The New Math

Suppose one of you wants to build a tower. Won't you first sit down and estimate the cost to see if you have enough money to complete it? — Luke 14:28

Most cashiers today don't know how to count down change from the cash they receive. Computers calculate the amount for them, and they count up to that number. Adding a quarter, nickel, and three pennies might be too much work. Those who are stressed with counting coins should be thankful that most people use credit cards.

Adding Numbers

Some college students bought watermelons for $2 and sold them for $1. After showing a loss in the first week of business, they were asked how they expected to stay in business. They did some creative accounting with their new math and found the solution. To break even, they would have to double their sales volume. That story is told as a joke, but when our politicians calculate that way, it isn't funny.

Should we listen to politicians when they say it's okay to spend more than they take in? Apparently, we are expected to believe we can collect two dollars in taxes, spend three dollars, and still have a dollar to spend on something else. All the right numbers are there, but we haven't correctly balanced the equation.

In school, I had to work math problems. *If you have five apples and give three to a friend, how many do you have left?* I used the think the correct answer was two. But with our new government calculations, if I'm rich enough to have five apples, I can't have but one. The government takes four, gives one to my friend, and somehow gives one to five strangers. In my old-school math, those numbers don't add up, but they do when we allow deficit spending. I'm told I should be happy with my one apple, because I own the orchard. I shouldn't be entitled to more than what others have.

With this kind of math, you might understand why I want to sell my orchard and get out of the apple business.

The Equal Sign

With a balanced equation, I should be able to compare the sum on each side of the equal sign and see that they match. Politicians don't like that approach, so they have to use a new approach to make the numbers work. How do they do it?

By ignoring the equal sign, politicians can make all kinds of promises without explaining where the money will come from. Supposedly, all the rich people and businesses will cough up the cash, but if that were to happen, the rich people will take their money to foreign countries that would like to have it on deposit. And if the businesses don't close their doors, employee layoffs or increased prices will have to offset loss.

Politicians may ignore the equal sign, but individuals and businesses cannot. That's because politicians get away with framing words and numbers in a way that people can believe they will get something for nothing. Businesses must face reality, not the way they would like the numbers to add up. They can't have more money going out than what they have coming in—at least not for very long.

I wonder how much longer our government can get away with not balancing the equation. We've had enough scary times in our history that we should be concerned.

Maybe we should go back to our old-fashioned values and require politicians to balance their expenditures with what they take in. Doing that would sure change the campaign rhetoric.

A Balanced Budget

Our national debt has steadily increased over the last hundred years. In the last ten years, the *rate* of increase has increased faster

182

than the weeds growing in my back yard. We seem to think we have a credit card with a no limit on how much can be spent each year.

If interest rates were not kept artificially low by our government, we would soon be unable to pay even the interest on our national debt. Apparently, most of our politicians like our new math, because they consistently resist any attempt to require a balanced budget. We do well to pass a budget at all.

If individuals never had to balance their check books with their bank statements, and their bank account would automatically increase an outstanding loan to cover whatever was spend above cash receipts, we'd have a situation that resembles what the government can do every day.

Old-Fashioned Arithmetic

My wife and I started budgeting soon after we were married. It was a pretty simple process using basic second-grade addition and subtraction. With each month's income, we decided how much would go to savings and how much could be spent. We knew the bank wouldn't let us overdraw the account using new math. We weren't like the government, able to print more money as needed.

If an unexpected expense arose, we had to cut back budgeted expenses even more. The numbers had to add up. Borrowing to cover monthly expenses is never smart, because the debt keeps growing until it's unsustainable. The only solution is to cut expenses.

Baseline Budgeting

One of the most deceptive ways politicians appear to cut spending uses the new math that actually allows increased spending. The baseline is set based on current and anticipated expenses adjusted for inflation. It's something like saying we spent $500 last year and expect to spend an additional $500 this year. But then we actually spend $750 and claim to have cut the budget by $250.

A wife said to her husband, "I saved $100 today." When asked how, she said, "Found a $250 dress marked down to $200, so I bought two." That kind of new math won't work well in a marriage. But if the federal government is allowed to make up its own accounting rules, it can deceive the voters into believing they are being fiscally prudent when they are actually spending too much.

Decreasing the Deficit

We've not reduced the deficit in a hundred years. In prosperous times when more individuals and businesses made money, more taxes were paid, but that hasn't reduced the deficit. Actually, what it has done is reduce the rate of the increase.

For example, if we added two trillion dollars to the debt last year and add one trillion this year, politicians might claim to have reduced the debt by 50 percent. They get away with saying things like that when the media won't expose their deception.

Wouldn't it be nice if we could return to our old-fashioned values of honesty and truth?

Bond Issues

Selling bonds can seem almost as good as buying a boat for nothing down and no payments due for ten years. Right now, we have lots of money we can spend, and it will be a long time before anyone has to worry about payment. By then, we might be flush with cash, but that's wishful thinking. It never works out that way.

Perhaps one reason so many voters will tolerate the new math is due to their own fiscal irresponsibility. I've read that seven out of ten Americans don't know when they'll ever get out of debt. So if you have ten dollars in your wallet and are debt free, you're living in an elite class of wealthy people. Those who have 401(k) plans built from payroll withholding will often have to borrow money from their accounts and will never pay it back. Almost half of Americans never put any of their paychecks into savings.

Tax the Rich

Our government leaders need to take a course in remedial math. Somehow they must have missed learning simple arithmetic in school. If the top 1 percent of American wage earners paid *all* their income in taxes, it wouldn't make a dent in our federal debt. Either our politicians can't do the math, or they're lying when they say it will.

184

I know that voters like to hear about the rich paying their bill for government benefits, but doing that could be problematic. There just isn't enough money to make that much difference. The truth is, if free healthcare and schooling ever become a reality, all taxpayers will be paying a lot more. Besides that, if we tax corporate leaders too heavily, countless workers could lose their jobs when the top skilled positions are abandoned.

Political Persuasion

Repeat a lie often enough and long enough and it becomes the truth. At that point, any straggler who disagrees is condemned without proof, just because "everyone" knows it's true.

Sometimes it becomes true only because we believe it, a self-fulling prophecy. Take the economy, for example. If the opposition party can make enough people believe the country is headed for collapse, people will cut back on spending, forcing businesses to reduce their workforce, increasing claims for unemployment, adding to welfare cries and media focus on demonstrations and riots. Sure enough, the politicians were right. The country is in trouble, so we need to elect or reelect the deceptive politicians who fabricate false news.

The new math works whenever politicians can spin the numbers and make them work. Spinning statistics to make a political point is easy. They just leave out the numbers that don't support the claim they want to make. Add media focus that doesn't question the argument, and a multitude may be convinced.

We have seen demonstrations and violent protests in dozens of cities claiming police brutality that wasn't true. But the violence, injured people, and businesses destroyed was real. The media covered it all, and when it turned out to be false, the media did little, if anything, to retract their bad coverage. Maybe it wasn't brutality in that one situation, but the spin was still justified because we all know that police brutality exists. That's why it's being investigated.

If we allow politicians to convict people by accusation, then no innocent person is safe from having their lives destroyed by false claims. Our new-fashioned values won't condemn politicians for lying. Their supporters embrace the claims, even when they know it's a lie, because it helps their agenda.

We need to take two old-fashioned truth pills, and maybe our country will be a little better in the morning.

Need for Good Numbers

For all the politicians who spin the numbers to say what they want, we need more than opposing arguments that seldom get air time. We need agencies and people who can add truth to perception and help us add two plus two and get the right answer.

Congress and governments at all levels should take an old-fashioned course on truth, justice, and what use to be "the American way." Universities and school districts need to throw out the text books with "new math." Even some churches could use a little remedial training.

I once talked with Walter Schloss, who was ninety-five years old at the time. Walter was a financial advisor and helped people produce some of the highest rates of return of anyone in that field. One of his key principles was to never buy a company that had too much debt. Other factors might look very good, but to make the right decisions, we need to know the true numbers and how to add them correctly. Walter had the right old-fashioned values.

I recommend a compass value selection called common sense. In the old days, we called it "horse sense," when it wasn't that hard to add the numbers and get the right answer.

Legalized Slavery

*Diligent hands will rule, but laziness ends
in forced labor.—Proverbs 12:24*

I hate slavery. For two centuries, America has been the land of the
free and home for the brave. But our new-fashioned values could
lead us into the kinds of government enslavement that our
ancestors fled.

Not a Pretty Picture

If this slavery was from southern plantation owners wielding whips,
abusing their workers who had nowhere to go, we would have seen
the problem coming. This picture is more deceptive, and that's
what makes it so ugly. Taxpayers are already paying a hefty price.
I'm talking about the modern form of slavery: our dependency on a
socialist-leaning government.

As more people are reduced to dependencies on subsidized
housing, food stamps, and other welfare support, I see Uncle Sam
as a cruel, deceptive taskmaster. If his power keeps growing, the
next picture will be worse than the old tobacco plantations where
so many slaved all day for barely enough to survive.

All this is happening under the guise of equal opportunity,
inclusion, and freedom from religion in which all are expected to
participate. I had no idea what this kind of slavery might look
like—until I became an eyewitness.

Indian Reservations

Years ago, I was involved in a business that harvested seed on
several Indian reservations. I saw firsthand what happened when

supposedly generous Uncle Sam took charge and reduced the Indian culture to government dependency. Areas of poverty, control of education, and use of alcohol were an eye opener for me. The Indians were oppressed from all sides by people who wanted to manipulate and exploit the situation to their advantage.

This was a socialism issue, not a matter of race. The government agents were of all colors and ethnic backgrounds—white, black, and brown. The dependents couldn't leave the reservation to pursue outside opportunities, which enslaved many good people in almost impossible situations. I believe it was Henry Ford who said people who think they can be happy and prosperous by letting the government take care of them should take a close look at what happened to the American Indian.

What I see happening now reminds me of those days. If it happened to them, it could happen to everyone who becomes too dependent upon the government.

Spiral of Dependency

Many good people have already fallen into the spiral of dependency and can't find their way out. I am sorry for so many Indians who never made it to the reservation, because they were killed. In a way, since the numbers of people involve the entire country, conditions seem even worse now.

Who is to blame for putting so many of our good people into this kind of slavery? Our uncle, good old Sam, started this diabolical process almost fifty years ago to "help" people who weren't doing enough to help themselves. The goal of this Great Society was to "eliminate poverty." Uncle Sam seemed like such a nice guy, we welcomed his program onto our reservations.

An Expensive War

Since the beginning of the War on Poverty, we've spent almost $20 trillion trying to give comfortable homes to all the poor of all races and ethnic backgrounds, even those who have entered the country illegally. Some are on drugs. Others are seldom sober. A few are criminal threats to our society.

Have we made conditions better with these dependencies on government support? Given the number and size of our homeless camps, apparently not. Whole communities have become disaster areas. Our new-fashioned values have made matters worse.

Sweet Intentions Turned Sour

Kindhearted Uncle Sam thought he could help poor people with free stuff—a place to live, food for the table. The idea sounded so good, everyone cheered. The media got support to spread the message. So did colleges and universities. "This is good, very good," they said. Progressives everywhere assured us that our country was now moving in the right direction—away from old-fashioned values to something new and better.

Sam gathered a crowd of helpers—the media, politicians, groups with their own self-serving agendas. The hustlers who profit are just like the people who took advantage of the Indians on the reservations. And their hustling grows the problem they are supposedly there to solve.

As it turns out, the new-fashioned values have turned sour, and we could use some of the old-fashioned sweetness.

Need for an Overhaul

Uncle Sam's dependency system is in bad need of repair. Politicians seem intent on doing more of what hasn't worked. Why? They want to stay in control, which is best achieved by giving voters more and more stuff to keep them in their state of legalized slavery, depending on the government, unable to leave the reservation to pursue new opportunities.

In many large cities, entire communities have been reduced to a state of dependency. The dysfunction is pretty much the same everywhere—with high poverty, poor living conditions, and crime. For the last fifty years, the same politicians keep promising them freedom from this enslavement, but their socialist system has accomplished the opposite, which keeps the hustlers in power.

Minority Indians

Whenever we allow Uncle Sam to have control of our lives, we can expect to be manipulated and used for someone else's profit, no matter what our color or ethnic background is. In this sense, we are a mixed breed of American Indians who are red, yellow, black, white, and brown. That is not to say that some races are not more enslaved than others, because clearly, some are.

Black folks account for about an eighth of the U.S. population. Many of our citizens have been in this country for enough generations to be part "black," even though that might not be apparent in their skin color. So I use the term loosely, not to offend, but to illustrate Uncle Sam's ability to constrain us on reservations and manipulate us.

In black communities, about 75 percent of babies are born to single-parent families, a number that has increased dramatically in the last twenty years. Teen pregnancy is three times the national average. These are perfect conditions for the government to step in with welfare that leaves the community enslaved in their dependency, unable to break into a land of opportunity.

Plantation Politics

The federal Aid to Families with Dependent Children assistance program (AFDC) has become a great invitation for residency on Uncle Sam's slavery plantation. This was not the original intent, but it has worked out that way, providing benefits for a rapidly increasing number of single moms. In some communities, an army of politicians encourage this form of dependency, sometimes with paid advertising.

What kind of culture is our socialism breeding? Rappers shout for more entitlements. Churches promote resentment for people not being given more. We're taught to feel sorry for ourselves and demand more help from our taskmasters. This effort is increasing our slavery, not reducing it.

Instead of promoting dependency, we need to strengthen families with the old-fashioned kind of faith and encouragement, leading people to break their bonds of slavery and escape to a life of success and opportunity.

190

Welcome Centers

The government's plantation can look good to people who don't mind the confinement and have little desire to make a better life for themselves. Uncle Sam is working hard to build plantations for all races, including illegal immigrants. He has a Welcome Wagon basket of goodies for new residents to receive as soon as they move in.

Some politicians want these communities to grow, because a vote from a person on welfare counts as much as a business owner. The plantation residents know how to work the system, getting maximum benefits from the government because they have no place of employment. Then they can supplement those benefits by panhandling, working for cash, or bartering—anything that puts tax-free cash in their hands without having it show up as income.

I'm not sure why Asian and European immigrants are less inclined to join the plantations communities. They seem to have different values that make them less interested in Uncle Sam's invitation. Instead, they love their freedom, study hard, and are more likely to be successful in business.

Try to find a program to improve life for black Americans that isn't government funded. You'll have to look hard, and you may never find one. The civil rights movement used to be about freedom and escape from the plantations. Now, all we've done is subject ourselves to a different taskmaster—the government dependency. We should be ashamed.

I remember Dr. Martin Luther King's dream. Blacks on the plantation, dependent on government welfare, wasn't it. What Dr. King wanted for the black community was straight from the old-fashioned-values textbook: equal opportunity for all races. We aren't all equal, as if God has made us carbon copies of one another. That's obvious. But we should have equal *opportunity*. The government welfare plantations are enslaving, depriving people of freedom and opportunity.

Outside the Plantation

If Dr. King could see conditions today, I think he would be both pleased and appalled. He wouldn't like the welfare communities and families struggling with a single parent at home. But he would be very proud of our progress toward equal opportunity in education, housing, and jobs opportunities and jobs outside the plantation.

He would be pleased that we don't segregate black people in the buses, water fountains, or restrooms. Outside the plantations, black people can excel in academics, sports, and business. They can hold important positions in the military, law enforcement, and government. But he would be most displeased with the politicians and community leaders who promote racism by focusing on the problems without offering solutions.

If Dr. King could speak to us today, I'm sure he would preach for equality in opportunity and harmony of all races. And he would do it peacefully, condemning violence and rioting. He would be encouraged because our still-imperfect world is now much better, but then he would be troubled, because our new socialist values are making matters worse, taking us back to the plantations.

Equal Opportunity

If we were all created equal, as our Declaration of Independence claims, then some people must be more equal than others. I think we should quit trying to be like others and instead recognize our unique strengths. Then, each of us could excel in our own special way.

Those who have used their abilities and have seized an opportunity to be successful deserve special praise. Government welfare is easy to achieve. Being successful is never easy. For those who leave the plantations, life can be exceptionally challenging, but every successful person will tell you that it was worth the effort. Our greatest treasures come at the highest costs.

People born into poverty follow a very difficult path. I think Dr. Martin Luther King would be extremely proud how many people of all races have broken barriers and climbed mountains to become responsible leaders in our society. They scrimped and saved, worked hard, and followed some old-fashioned values in raising good children who will become tomorrow's leaders. Perhaps he looked down from Heaven with pride, seeing America inaugurate its first black president. He would be delighted to see so many minorities in education, business, the military, and government positions.

I know our society still has a few racist dimwits who don't believe in equal opportunity, and I'm sorry that they get so much more publicity than the multitudes who care for one another. The news coverage and political bantering gives racism more coverage than it deserves.

I'm all for the media focusing on the problem, even though the close-up views can make molehills look like mountains. Those who are hurting are not imagining their pain. It's real, and they need help. The problem I have is with the media and many politicians who stay focused on the problem to increase their power and their own prosperity. They make socialism promises that won't work while avoiding the solutions that would work.

Prayer and Prejudice

Some of our great church hymns were birthed among the slave culture on the southern plantations. Needy people have a reason to trust God, pray, and sing about their faith. God never missed a word. He heard the cries of his people and delivered them from Egypt. And the slavery that had been part of the world culture for thousands of years came to an end after the Civil War. Racial prejudice continued for another hundred years.

In advancing his message, Dr. King preached non-violence. He would not be happy with the race hustlers and political leaders who condone rioting and looting, who feed upon the anger they stir up for their own power and prosperity. He would be appalled to hear chants like "pigs in a blanket, fry them like bacon."

I wonder what Dr. King would say to pastors who damn America, condemn the Jews, and encourage segregation? He might say, "Why didn't you listen to what I was preaching?" We have come a long way, but our new-fashioned socialist values promoted in recent years have us slipping a bit.

The Slave Trade

If we expect everyone to be kind and generous, we're not good judges of human nature. I'm sure our legislators from decades past never dreamed that politicians would one day use government welfare to boost their power and prosperity and enslave people in their dependencies.

When people are brave enough to denounce the abuse in our welfare communities, they are branded as racist. Somehow, the media often wants to promote those accusations, as if they are true, when actually it's more true of the accusers who are engaged in a new-fashioned kind of slave trade.

Change of Heart

Uncle Sam could use some heart surgery to restore some of the old-fashioned values for quality education, faith in God, and equal opportunity with less government control. Welfare should be reserved for the needy, not those who prefer living at the poverty level with government handouts so they don't have to work.

We should support programs for education, opportunity, and success, but avoid recruiting for the plantation and gaining votes for politicians. A better program would mandate work for benefits.

Global Warming

He causes his sun to rise on the evil and the good, and sends rain on the righteous and the unrighteous. — Matthew 5:45

Climate has been changing for millennia, ever since the Great Flood, after Noah waited for the waters to recede. Long before we learned to pump oil and gas and put cars on the road, weather patterns have been changing, sometimes turning forests into deserts.

Nothing New

When I was in high school, I heard Jim Castle, my vocational agriculture teacher, say that the climate had changed significantly in predictable cycles over thousands of years. He called these cycles "climate change." He said scientists had traced the cycles and had written about these changes for thousands of years.

This was many decades before politicians saw an opportunity to get rich and made it such a big deal. The truth didn't matter, which Al Gore made obvious with his claims that have proven not to be true. He claimed to be an "expert" on global warming. He didn't invent the Internet. Actually, he is a "promoter" of global warming, better qualified than the best "snake oil" salesman.

Coming Ice Age

A few years after Jim Castle's weather history lesson, we were warned that an ice age was coming, an alarmist prediction that civilization as we knew it would come to an end. We did have some bitterly cold winters. Many record low temperatures were set, but all the Texas lakes didn't freeze over.

After reaching the low point in the cycle, we didn't suddenly put more cars on the road or increase our herds of farting cows. But with the temperatures going up, instead of predicting a country frozen in ice, alarmists said the planet would soon be destroyed because of global warming.

Climate Change

When I heard Jim Castle teach, he didn't know that scientists with the National Academy of Science would pretty much agree that changes in CO_2 would cause our climate to change. He hadn't used the term "global warming," and he had no idea that this condition would later be renamed to what he referred to as the normal cycle of "climate change."

The "global warming" term wasn't making good sense when the South was covered in snow. There was one day in winter when somewhere in all fifty states, snow was on the ground. To avoid having too many doubts about global warming, the politically correct term for common use became "climate change."

People had no problem believing our climate was changing. For centuries, we've seen hot and cooler days than usual. Droughts have been broken by floods, and floods ended with periods of drought. With widespread public acceptance, we could blame just about every evil thing on climate change. If we had more storms in the spring or if it was exceptionally dry, if we had more hurricanes in the Atlantic or we had way less than predicted, if winters were mild or harsh—it didn't matter. Everybody knew that the unusual, unpredictable aspects of weather and fluctuations of sea temperatures were due to climate change.

With the help of politicians and the media we learned of the problem. No longer could we be content with predicting the weather. We needed to change it.

Clean Air

As an advocate of clean air and water, Jim Castle was ahead of his time in wanting to eliminate smog and do recycling. He supported crop rotation and use of natural fertilizer. He wanted to conserve water, and thought we should clean up our rivers, lakes, and oceans. He was a "green" guy before it was popular to be one.

Jim could never have imagined how divided our climate-change views could be, but then he didn't anticipate what politicians and the media could do to polarize people's beliefs. He just wanted us to be good farmers, value and conserve our resources, and keep our environment clean.

Carbon Emissions

My Vocational Ag teacher did not know all the so-called scientific evidence that exists today showing the world burning up because of carbon emissions. Jim thought CO_2 was pretty good stuff for plants to grow and to synthesize oxygen for humans and animal life. He thought cow poop made a good fertilizer. Still, I think Jim would agree that we need to clean up our act in some areas.

We now have the country in a dither, with news and weather focused on every time we're above average. Whenever it's below average, we have no reason to mention anything that might suggest that our forecasts of coming doom might be inaccurate. We see melting ice on top of glaciers, which happens every summer, but it gives us a picture of conditions getting worse. We need to show the crops burning up in Africa, which is nothing new, but it emphasizes the point. Polar bears don't know it, but they are about to become extinct.

We'll soon be able to fry eggs on the sidewalk. We'll face terrible floods, which has always been happening somewhere, but we need the pictures to stoke our fears. Global warming causes terrorism. That's why we have more sharks biting swimmers and why wild animals are more vicious. We should worry about the squirrels in our yards. They might attack because of global warming.

Obvious Truth

Now that "everyone" knows the truth, alarmists and the media can attack scientists and anyone else who disagrees, branding them as just ignorant or stupid. Everybody knows we have climate change, so only an idiot would look at statistics and disagree. Why would these dumb people raise questions when everybody knows the world is about to end?

I've read that carbon dioxide comprises only .04 percent of our atmosphere. Some measurements say that number reflects an increase of 25 percent, which sounds like a big number, but it's actually a rise of .03 to .04, an increase of one hundredth of 1 percent. Since the temperatures are up, alarmists conclude that the increase in CO_2 levels must be the cause. All our gas-guzzling cars need to go electric, which sounds right, since everybody has heard that so many times. But the "idiots" say the politicians have it backward. What they think is a cause is actually an effect. Because the temperatures have gone up as a part of the normal cycle of climate change, the CO_2 levels have naturally gone up. If driving our cars has had any effect at all, it isn't much. And saying cow poop makes a difference in the climate is absurd.

As it turns out, our obvious truth isn't as obvious as some politicians would have us believe.

Alarmist Profits

Businesses to combat global warming are among the most powerful enterprises today. Professors, scientists, actors, newscasters, authors, and politicians have a vested interest in maintaining and promoting this profitable industry. The movie *An Inconvenient Truth* was heavily promoted to make a lot of people rich. Very rich.

Former Vice President Al Gore has increased his net worth by several hundred million dollars as a Global Warming Promoter (GWP), which allows him to live in a gigantic CO_2 belching mansion, drive big old nasty carbon-emitting SUVs, and fly around the world in jumbo jets to speak about climate change. I'm guessing he also eats beef.

Third-world countries benefit because world organizations demand the biggest offending nations pay the smaller nations for not polluting as much.

Volcanic Eruptions

If Jim Castle were alive today, I have no doubt he would raise the issue of volcanic eruptions. In four days, the eruption in Iceland released more emissions than we have been able to curb with our global warming initiatives in five years. When Mount Pinatubo erupted in the Philippines in 1991, more greenhouse gases were released into the atmosphere than what the human race has produced since mankind first walked on Earth. I've heard that the Mount Etna eruption spewed ten thousand times more than that. And we're supposed to believe automobiles are a factor? Give me a break.

If we were serious about the problem, we should develop technology to contain the eruptions, but that wouldn't be politically expedient. Politicians and alarmists wouldn't get rich on that venture.

Cap and Trade

Some politicians tried to pass a law that would penalize companies that exceeded stringent standards for how much CO_2 could be released into the air. If it had passed and became law, prices would have gone up to cover the increased cost. Some business would have closed their doors. Potentially thousands of jobs would have been lost.

But the law would have been wonderful for the global warming agenda, because functionally it was a hidden tax that put lots of money into government hands to fund more welfare benefits. No matter that it would have cost Americans hundreds of billions of dollars a year in higher prices.

We were told that production of Ethanol was a wonderful means to curb carbon emissions. Billions of taxpayer dollars subsidized the industry, making some politicians and alarmists very rich at taxpayer expense. The price of gas didn't go down, and the price of corn went up, as well as beef, pork, chicken, and cornflakes.

Consensus Proof

The alarmists talk like life on Earth will soon end if we don't run all our cars and trucks on electricity. They say anybody who doesn't agree is against science, because 99 percent of scientists know that the increased CO_2 levels are responsible for global warming. When the media supports that message, because they are either too lazy to research the truth or are unwilling to question the claim, most people think 99 percent sounds about right and are led to believe it must be true.

What is it, really? I'm guessing that 99 percent of the scientists who work for the government say it's true. But I've read that independent research groups have surveyed scientists and found that at least 50 percent, maybe more, don't think the global warming claims are valid.

Public Education

Abraham Lincoln supposedly said, "You can fool all the people some of the time and some of the people all the time, but you cannot fool all the people all the time." I don't know if he really said that, but I'm sure he wasn't referring to children. All young, innocent minds are like sponges, soaking up whatever they're told. Since they've not learned to think for themselves, all of them can be fooled all the time.

Since children accept propaganda as absolute truth, public schools can teach global warming as fact, frightening them with apocalyptic climate scenarios based on shoddy science and unproved assumptions. With the support of government and biased scientists, they seem to be doing a very good job of that.

Global Deception

Hundreds of millions of dollars are being spent on international conferences, technology, and programs to promote this global-warming cause. Much of this comes with government support, and you should know what that means. Taxpayers are funding much of the deception.

We should not underestimate the power of the media, not just across our country but also around the world. When the public is constantly bombarded with a message and opposing views are excluded, most people are inclined to believe what they see and hear.

Deplorable Idiots

When lawmakers and old-fashioned folks like me challenge the propaganda, they are ridiculed as ignorant and unscientific. The media has been able to silence the opposition for so long that getting a voice anywhere is virtually impossible. When I raise the issue among friends, they usually shake their heads and turn away, as if I am obviously out of touch with reality.

I think my high school agriculture teacher made more sense than what the global warming profiteers are selling. Millions of others feel the same way, but they are either afraid to speak up or are given no publicity when they do.

Cost of Diversion

Taking the wrong road may seem right, but it's an unnecessary cost in getting where you want to go. When the fuel pump has failed, the car won't run with a tune-up. That's not to say a tune-up is bad, but it's not a good use of financial resources.

The proponents of global warming seem to be against all energy production that is necessary to keep the world going. Their bias goes far beyond practicality and reason, which might not be surprising if they can think cow poop is as consequential as volcanic eruptions. If they could be realistic in costs, they would know that solar and wind energy will not be the saviors of mankind.

I love clean air and water, so I'm all for reducing smog and cutting emissions. I've traveled to countries where pollution was such a problem that I wondered why anyone would want to live there. Breathing that stuff day and night cannot be healthy.

I resent the politicians and alarmists who have made global warming a problem bigger than it really is, for the benefit of power and profit. If we could apply some of my old-fashioned values and question the motives of those who might be twisting the truth, we could step back and take an objective look at what really is broken and needs to be fixed.

Gone Wild

"I have the right to do anything," you say—but
not everything is beneficial.—1 Corinthians 6:12

I agree with President Ronald Reagan assessment of our
government's view of the American economy: "If it moves, tax it.
If it keeps moving, regulate it. And if it stops moving, subsidize it."

Spring Break

Teenagers are known for abandoning their sense of values during
spring break, going wild. Some of our government leaders seem to
have gone crazy year-round, as if they think it's spring break all the
time.

Our governments weren't always an enemy to free enterprise,
but our new values encourage it, because we're so easily deceived
into thinking businesses pay taxes. We call it that, but actually *people*
pay taxes, which makes their take-home pay smaller. The taxes that
businesses pay are costs that raise their costs of goods or services
sold, so *people's* take-home pay won't buy as much.

The wild time isn't just from the federal government. Cities,
states, and counties have joined the fun, not just taxing citizens
directly but also indirectly, by charging businesses with taxes and
fees.

Inflated Costs

When my wife and I said our marriage vows, a dollar would buy
more than five gallons of gas. Now, it might not buy a quart. We
could pay the doctor his $10 fee or trade him a chicken. A first-
class letter could be mailed for three cents. A nickel could buy a

candy bar that now costs a dollar. I'm not sure why we have pennies. If it were legal to melt them down, we could sell pennies for almost double their cost.

Our government ran pretty smooth back then, with debt a little over $250 billion. Now, the debt is almost a hundred times higher, more than $22 trillion. If you think the average American is making a lot more money now, guess again. Whenever wages go up, so do the costs of goods and services. And so do taxes. If the tax rate stays the same and your wages go up 10 percent, and your deductions stay the same, your taxes will go up by more than the original 10 percent, because it's a percentage of a larger number. If someone were making $10 per hour, and the new job paid $30, you might think the take-home pay would be triple. But no, the more you make, the more the government takes.

I'm not sure how much longer our government can continue its wild spending and skyrocketing debt, and keep inflation under control.

Student Loans

When my wife and I decided to go back to college in 1955, we had a baby at home and little money. In those days, scholarships didn't amount to much—maybe $100 if you were the high school valedictorian. Student loans were unheard of. Request for a bank loan without collateral would get nothing but laughter, because the government wasn't promoting student loan programs that would never be repaid.

Most people out of high school had to work their way through college, so you might guess that they were going for the education, not to party and have fun.

Our values told us that we should stay away from trying to get something for nothing. Borrowing from the future, even if we could have done that, wasn't popular. The pay-as-you-go plan was better, so we scrimped and saved, depriving ourselves of many pleasures and conveniences.

We now live in a day when credit has gone wild. People buy just about everything on credit, seldom considering the financial strain for paying later. They may have several loans and max out their credit cards until their payments take most of their paychecks.

With the government's encouragement, student loan debt is over $1.5 trillion and soaring, with millions of borrowers in default, either unwilling or unable to repay their debts. If our government became really wild, it should use the socialist approach, forgive all the debt, and make college free. Promising that to students and the forty-five million debtors would be sure to get lots of votes and make many parents and grandparents happy, but I don't know how taxpayers could ever pay for that.

Protests

We could debate whether life today is better than it used to be. That might depend on the country and locality where you live. The industrial age and advances in technology has certainly given us machines, transportation, and communication that was only a part of dreams a hundred years ago.

We don't have to look very far to see that the world is not a very happy place. A hundred years ago, we didn't know about gangs and terrorists. People had guns, but they didn't go around shooting everyone in schools and churches. We used to see protests and riots in foreign countries, especially where radical socialist governments were in control, but now we're having to deal with them in our own country.

Perhaps what we're seeing is what happens with socialist governments as their leaders become super rich making promises to take care of everybody's needs, and then they run out of other people's money. Not getting their entitlements, the people go wild.

Begging for Attention

The next presidential election is sure to bring fresh waves of wild promises, without the media questioning how people who vote for these candidates will feel after their expectations can't be met. Some people question exorbitant political promises with no plausible means for funding more free benefits. Nevertheless, about half our country wants the government to be even wilder, not less.

Why do riots happen? Many reasons have been given, including poverty, unemployment, reduced services, police brutality, and racial tension. Actually, mobs form behind leaders. Without organizers to stir people to violence, most people would stay at home. With politicians and celebrity activists screaming about injustices, telling people they've been mistreated, that they should be given more, and with the media constantly stirring the "get wild" pot, organizers use social media to easily gather a mob of fanatics demanding action, ready to hang anybody who doesn't agree with them.

Terrorists obviously don't care about the people they kill or the property they destroy. What do they care about? Mostly, it's the media coverage. And we're just crazy enough to quit giving it to them. Remember the streaking fad where someone would run naked across the field to get attention? Rarely does that happen today. Do you know why? Morality didn't suddenly acquire old-fashioned values. I think we ruined their motivation by refusing to give them media coverage.

When people go wild for attention, one of the best things we can do is deprive them of any media attention.

Government Guarantees

I think some politicians and media have convinced much of our society that people should be guaranteed a standard of living, even if they are illegal immigrants. My old-fashioned values said I wasn't entitled to anything without making sacrifices and doing lots of hard work. I was never part of a group that thought the government owed me a minimum standard of living. Success was made the old-fashioned way. We earned it.

Today, many have gone wild over not being sufficiently rewarded for living in this country. Many popular politicians agree, saying Wall Street and all the rich people are depriving them of their rights. Supposedly, if the rich were paying their fair share, they could have free college, free healthcare, free housing, free food, and free phones. I don't know how many people actually believe they could have all that, but there's no doubt they expect the government to give them more.

Brought to a Slow Boil

How did we get to the unhappy state of malaise, riots, demonstrations, and disrespect for our government and one another that we see today? Perhaps our government has "gone too wild" with socialist promises. This change didn't just happen overnight.

Compare today's picture to fifty years ago, and you will see a dramatic difference in both people's entitlements and what the government is expected to give. Politicians have bought votes by appealing to about every desire and whim that good advertising and marketing can produce. This dependency on government has come at a very high cost to the taxpayer.

The pot is still boiling. Politicians are feverishly working to create new "plantations" to enslave more people under government welfare, healthcare, and other dependencies.

Young people feel cheated by the government if they can't go to college and be assisted with loans, subsidies, easy classes, and "safe places." When I was young, high school graduates didn't think they were entitled to a college education. That was something to be earned with hard work. Nobody thought it should be free. Trade schools and apprenticeships were a big option back then.

Unemployment

When unemployment peaked during the Obama administration, we did more to encourage people not to work. The government went wild with increasing unemployment benefits. People are sometimes smarter than what the government gives them credit for. They could add the numbers. If the available jobs paid about the same or sometimes less than the unemployment benefits, people lost their interest in working.

Employment cutbacks are a natural reaction when the government adds rules that restrict the market and raise costs for goods and services, then add more fees and taxes. Do we think boosting unemployment benefits will create more jobs and boost employment? Subsidizing businesses doesn't work, because we're just shuffling tax money from one place to another. In effect, to help the hurting businesses, they take money from other business so everyone can hurt. We were better off in the old days with our old-fashioned values, when businesses could grow without fighting the government.

Bloated Bureaucracy

Government employees can typically work less hours with less effort and still make about 30 percent more than employees in the private sector. Government pensions are sometimes so lucrative that retirees can receive more than when they were working.

While unions in the private sector have bled business to the point they can barely survive, unions representing government employees continue to make gains. Politicians are only too eager to accept union demands in exchange for more votes.

If businesses in the private sector need more employees to do the work, managers must have the financial resources to pay them. But when more effort is needed in government agencies, managers have much more liberty to just hire more people, without much concern for experience or productivity.

We're almost wild enough in our thinking to hire illegal immigrants to work for the government and do nothing.

Demographics

With lower birth rates and less immigration, the white population in America has been steadily declining. The Hispanic, Asian, and Middle-Eastern minorities have risen dramatically, which wouldn't matter under our old-fashioned values where race and culture didn't matter. Back then, we were all Americans. But now, the media likes to separate colors and beliefs and put them to war with one another.

This country was formed a republic with a representative form of government, not a democracy controlled by whatever insanity might be popular with the voters. For centuries, we expected our representatives to do what was good for the country as a whole, but now we seem more concerned with satisfying special interest groups that influence the most votes. As a consequence, we can give more favorable press coverage for a 3 percent minority opinion while doing nothing for the 97 percent. We're letting the tail wag the dog, when it should be the other way around.

This is a pretty scary situation. When governments go wild making promises and buying votes, we have reason to be concerned about our country's future.

Silent Majority

Our country was founded upon principles different from what we're seeing today. Many of those values may not be known to the young generations, but those who have not yet turned thirty are still greatly outnumbered by those who are older and wiser. We just need to make our voices heard.

A majority of our population still wants leadership that will require our government to live within its means. At one time, we had a government by and for the people. Maybe we can see that again, but it won't be easy. We might need to do something more than pray.

Graveside Services

*"I am the resurrection and the life. The one who believes
in me will live, even though they die; and whoever lives
by believing in me will never die." — John 11:25–26*

We used to have a saying about our freedoms. We could sit on the
riverbank and fish all day. If we didn't want to do something, we
didn't have to—except one thing: we couldn't choose not to die.
Oh, and one more thing: before we die, we have to pay taxes.

After-Death Taxes

Our government seems to believe that our taxes should live on
after we die. With my old-fashioned values, I have trouble with
politicians spending taxpayer money like it was theirs. They seem to
have a very special talent for spending other people's money.

I am even more bothered by the idea that my assets should be
taxed when my hard-earned dollars are passed on to my heirs.
Taxes were already paid on those dollars, and the government
would like to collect again, after I die.

Lowering Taxes

I believe it was Winston Churchill who once said there was nothing
the government could give me that hadn't first been taken from
me. When I heard a past president say that lowering taxes was like
taking money from the government, I was more than a *little* upset.

They were saying it would be stealing from the government if I
had to pay less taxes. I knew where that argument was heading.
They were just a few sentences away from saying I ought to be

paying more—and I would be stealing from the government if I complain about paying my fair share.

Fair-Share Taxation

A government that is "by and for the people" should have something to say about how much they can be taxed and how those dollars are spent.

Unfortunately, our voting voice is weakened because over 40 percent of the population pays no income tax at all. I don't blame them for voting to tax the rich. I blame the system that allows "taxation without representation."

When I hear politicians say rich people are not paying their fair share, I wonder how it can be fair for almost half our citizens to pay no income tax at all. Not a dime. I believe our new-fashioned values are asking for more than a fair share from the rich, so most voters don't feel threated by having to pay something.

We will never have "fair share" taxation until the government quits hiding taxes in house payments, sales taxes, licensing fees, and levies against businesses. We can only know what we're actually paying if the tax code is changed where all individuals pay only a share of their incomes.

The Lottery Game

Before we argue that the lower-income families are being treated fairly when they pay nothing, we should consider what percentage of their finances go to food, lodging, and other essentials. Studies have clearly shown that poor people are the leading participants in buying lottery tickets. It seems that no matter how little they have, they can spare a little to bet on lottery games, even though there is virtually no chance of their winning.

The government takes advantage of this by taxing the lottery. The government takes about 40 percent, while a few lucky souls share the 60 percent that is again taxed at 25 percent.

Some people with old-fashioned values still think gambling is a sin, but the government overcame those prejudices by saying these funds would go toward improving education. Some of the money does, but not all of it. The funds that go to education give the

210

government even more control, teaching our children the value of socialism.

Hidden Taxes

In many years of my work history, I paid as much as 50 percent to the IRS and for state and local taxes. That was by no means *all* that I was paying—and I'm still paying. If the government wasn't able to hide so many taxes, our entire population might be screaming, "Unfair!"

Let's just look at some of the taxes being paid by businesses and by individuals: accounts receivables, building permits, CDL licenses, cigarettes, corporate income, dog licenses, excise taxes, federal income, federal unemployment, fishing and game licenses, food licenses, fuel permits, gasoline, inheritance, inventory, IRS interest charges, IRS penalties, liquor, luxury items, marriage licenses, Medicare, personal property, business property, real estate, service charges, Social Security, road usage, recreational vehicles, sales at retail, school, state income, state unemployment, telephone taxes and fees fee, utility taxes, vehicle license registration, vehicle sales taxes, watercraft registration, well permits, workers compensation taxes, airport fees and taxes, transportation tolls and taxes. Can you keep track of them all and know what you're actually paying each year? Maybe an accountant could do that, but most people can't.

When I rented a car in Phoenix, the combined taxes and fees (which are really taxes) totaled almost 50 percent of the total cost. In other cities, the percentage of car rental cost has been even higher. The government seems to be constantly looking for another way to collect a hidden tax.

Bond Packages

A lot of money was spent on advertising a billion-dollar bond package for the city. It promised that if it passed, taxes wouldn't have to be raised. Wonderful. But I'm wondering where the money came from to pay for that advertising. And who would be paying the interest on those bonds? As always, our taxes. We know this, because without some form of taxation and fee collection, the city would have no money.

This measure didn't keep me from paying more taxes. In the last three years, my city, county, and school taxes increased by over 40 percent, not by increasing the tax rate but by increasing the appraised value of my home.

These taxes will continue long after I am gone. Someone will be paying them.

Razzle Dazzle

Every time I turn around, I hear a political spin on taxation. I may be told that the rich people will be paying, as if the middle class and retired senior citizens will be exempt. They may say the taxes aren't going up. They might even go down. But it's the rate that will go down as inflation pushes property values up. If I look carefully, I'll see where the actual taxation went up instead of down.

Taxation is like a marriage with no opportunity for divorce, and there seems to be no "till death do us part" option. Even after I'm gone, somebody will be paying taxes for whatever assets I leave behind.

Debt Debate

The national debt doesn't go down. We keep pushing it up year after year, looking for future generations to make the tax payments that will at least pay the interest. The only thing that has gone down over the years is the rate of increase.

Occasionally, politicians express concern about the debt, but they never seem to sell the idea that expenses should be reduced, and especially not any of the treasured government benefits. Invariably, they point to the necessity of raising taxes, the most popular being those that the public doesn't see as affecting them.

The value of this increase is widely publicized as necessary and affordable because of the added benefits the country will provide. We can have free collage, free healthcare, better education, and more benefits for illegal immigrants.

I'm all for a balanced budget, but our politicians can't tolerate any proposal that would cut benefits to their voter base. So we keep playing the game of increasing debt and finding ways to make it appear that the "other guys" will be paying the tax bill. What they really want to do is redistribute all the wealth, but they will never admit that.

An Equitable Solution

The solution is way too simple for politicians to effectively argue the points, because it would eliminate all the hidden taxes. If no taxes were hidden, and the actual tax was itemized on their purchases, people would be shocked. And probably very angry. That's why I don't hold out much hope for a consumption tax that should actually be less than what we're currently paying if we include all the hidden taxes and fees.

A fair and just approach would be a "consumption tax." Everybody pays the same percentage. Those who have less money buy fewer goods and pay less. The rich people who buy multi-million dollar houses, airplanes, stocks, bonds, or anything else pays the same percentage, which might be more than what billionaires are paying now. But it would be fair to everyone.

For example, let's suppose the consumption tax was 5 percent. A low-income person makes $20 thousand per year and spends it all. At 5 percent, he pays $1 thousand. If a billionaire makes $10 million a year, all that buying and selling of houses, land, stocks, and bonds could easily amount to 5 percent of $500 million, or $25 million in consumer taxes. Both the rich and the poor have the same option: Save tax by spending less. Have more by paying more tax. So the rich who have more and want more will be paying the lion's share of tax.

What is most fair about this approach to taxation is the closing of all the tax loopholes and the elimination of any need for filing tax returns. No more costs for accountants and lawyers to help the rich avoid taxes. No more opportunities for people to cheat on their taxes, either. Even the lottery can pay more to those who love to gamble, because the government won't get their huge cut. Everyone has a choice, whether to spend or save money, but everybody pays their fair share when they do.

Unavoidable Truth

Politicians are masters at twisting lies into something that sounds true, because we want to believe it. But here's the truth as it really is:

- The poor cannot be freed by imprisoning the wealthy.
- What one person receives without working is paid for by depriving workers a reward for their effort.
- The government can't give anything to anybody without first taking from someone else.
- When half the people think they don't have to work and the other half thinks it does no good to work, that nation cannot survive.
- Wealth cannot be multiplied by dividing it.
- We do well to respect Jesus' advice, everyone paying "Caesar" what he is due, and giving God what belongs to him (Matthew 22:21).

The national debt doesn't end with a person's death. Someone else will have to pay.

Problem Management

*The wise heart will know the proper time and
procedure. For there is a proper time and procedure
for every matter, though a person may be weighed
down by misery. — Ecclesiastes 8:5–6*

Problem Management

The wise heart will know the proper time and procedure. For there
is a proper time and procedure for every matter, though a person
may be weighed down by misery. — Ecclesiastes 8:5–6

The way our country manages problems today is nothing like the
way I ran successful companies. Maybe we should consider some of
the old-fashioned values that worked for me, because many times I
see the government's involvement making matters worse, not
better.

Management Experience

Lawyers may have many years of experience in the courts, handling
legal issues, but that doesn't do much toward learning how to
effectively run a business for profit. When lawyers can charge $250
to $1,000 per hour for their services, they don't have to worry
about profit. They can pay for luxury offices without concern for
the cost, and they seem to use a similar philosophy in running the
government.

I spent over fifty years in business, making key decisions. I soon
learned the necessity of cutting costs and improving profits
necessary to grow a business. I was president of several companies.
In many of my "retirement" years, I consulted with start-ups and
had to directly intervene with "problem" companies. Turning some

of these companies was like trying to guide a stampeding elephant. Three companies filed for bankruptcy and had to reorganize, and two others were nearly there. Having the right values is crucial for staying in business.

Fatal Problems

No business ever began with a plan to go bankrupt. They expected to make money, or they wouldn't have invested their time and money. They had a good product or service, so they could see no reason why they wouldn't be highly successful. What went wrong? Several key factors were typical:

- The service or product declined, so market share was lost.
- Employees were interested in serving themselves, not customers.
- More was being spent than the cash that was coming in, leaving budgets that couldn't be met.
- Assuming that everything would work out, managers failed to adjust to changing market demands.
- Poor performance was excused as just being "normal."
- Borrowing money to pay expenses added to the loss, creating more expense.

Our government has followed a similar self-destructive path for a long time.

Political Posturing

With some creative accounting, financial spreadsheets are easily manipulated with "new math" to satisfy the board and shareholders. A rosy picture of the future is painted to solicit loans for less-than-realistic growth plans.

Whenever a company keeps burying itself deeper in debt, it will inevitably pass a point of no return, where financial covenants cannot be met. Money borrowed to grow the business becomes insufficient to cover current operating expenses.

With systems failures within the business ignored, the chief executive office becomes the "campaigner in chief," a master politician to restructure loans and get concessions that keep the company afloat without making essential changes in operations. Government leaders today spend more time on political posturing, campaigning for re-election than they spend on taking care of government business, making the changes necessary to make the country strong financially, socially, and economically—both at home and abroad.

Misguided Profit

When the top management and board of directors become more concerned with their salaries and stock values than the company's ability to serve its customers, the business is headed for trouble.

Typically, the accounting is slanted to make the company look as good as possible, stretching the limits of the law and sometimes going beyond that, so the stock price will go up and bonuses and salaries can be justified. Managers and directors rejoice until the crisis shows up like a wolf at the boardroom door.

This sure seems like the way our government is being run—except the accounting goes far beyond anything that might be considered legal in the private sector. The rich rewards in high government salaries, pensions, consulting arrangements, and other perks are completely out of control. Taxpayers are paying for all this, but our voting shareholders who think they have nothing to lose seem to like that. They keep voting for the same leaders to give away more "dividends" on profits that don't exist.

Inevitable Failure

Bureaucracy is probably the biggest issue with problem businesses. The same is true for government enterprises—but on a much larger scale. Billion-dollar annual losses by the U.S. Postal Service is a good example.

Cronyism is also an issue in business, with managers wanting to reward family and close friends. Wanting to reward people for campaign support and contributions to a particular party, elected politicians hire people based on relationships, not ability and experience in the area where they will be working.

The problem companies usually have chief executive officers who can charm their boards of directors. They seem always able to say the right things, with little accountability for the company's performance. This is a practice that politicians have made a unique skill, where the most charismatic are elected, not those with the most ability to lead a country.

Bankruptcy

Unsuccessful companies must file for bankruptcy or go out of business. Some will file, reorganize, and fail again. Will our government ever have to file for bankruptcy? It should at least be recognized for doing its best to become bankrupt. If it continues its present path toward socialism values, the government taking everything but still unable to satisfy the people with everything they want, bankruptcy may be inevitable.

With the fed's help, our government can create money out of thin air and devalue currency so the debt can be paid with worthless dollars. Even so, I think there is a limit to how much this country can sustain in poor management, low productivity, and soaring debt.

The Root Problem

I'd like to blame the politicians for their mismanagement and greed. If they cared more for the country than their cash, members of Congress would work together to enact laws consistent with our Constitution. The people would hear the painful truth instead of what they want to believe, but right now that appears to be an impossible dream. The media won't support that change, and neither will the people with their new-fashioned values, wanting more free stuff.

I believe the root problem rests with the people who have allowed God and prayer to be removed from our education system, replaced by a warped morality that denies God's existence. Politicians and the media are able to twist the truth and fabricate lies because that's what people want to hear. If the younger generations that endorse political correctness and inclusiveness are able to exclude our old-fashioned values and rewrite our

Constitution to give government leaders complete control, then we are worse than bankrupt. We will be a failed nation like the ancient Roman Empire, unable to reorganize and rebuild.

I pray that God and our old-fashioned values will be recalled to bring us to our senses. We need leaders who will understand why "problem companies" fail and apply those principles to our government. Otherwise, our grandchildren will inherit an impossible mess.

A New Earth

Then I saw "a new heaven and a new earth," for the first heaven and the first earth had passed away, and there was no longer any sea. — Revelation 21:1

It may seem that I want to go back to the good old days, but that is not the case. Returning to the "good old days" would not be good. We just need to admit the mistakes we have made, restore the good principles we have lost, and return to our faith in God and country, and care for our fellow Americans more than ourselves. We would then have something greater than ever before.

A Complex World

Compared to fifty years ago, this world may seem as complex as it could ever be, but as time goes on, it will become even more complicated. My grandchildren will face more challenges than I ever had. But if they build their lives on Christian principles and treat others with respect, even their enemies, they will probably have more opportunities than I have ever had.

Without God's help, we wouldn't know how to read a moral compass, let alone see it calibrated correctly. For that, we pray a lot—and then do our best.

Progress

Even those in poverty, who are content with living on government support, would like to see progress. I am all for life getting better. The state of our nation right now gives me reason to be discouraged. We've talked a lot about that. But I'm also thankful for all the progress I've seen in the last eighty years.

In many ways, life is a lot better now. I grew up in a poor family, in a rural community. My father could not read or write. We did not have electricity, paved roads, or indoor plumbing. Our "toilet paper" was pages torn from catalogs and newspapers. Feed sacks were sometimes recycled to make dresses. Most kids went barefoot in the summer. Now, we can't imagine what life would be like without television, air conditioning, and cell phones.

With all the changes I've seen in just the last ten years, I cannot imagine what our country will be like in another twenty years. I hope these changes will be good, but that will depend on our values, whether they improve or get worse.

Think Tank

Almost fifty years ago, I worked for a large company that was concerned about the future. Since "strategic planning" was really important to us, I joined a task force of about a dozen people to anticipate what changes would take place in the next twenty years— a kind of "think tank."

We met day after day, looking at history and measuring trends. What "impossibilities" might actually be possible? How would technological advances change the market? If our company was to make the right strategic decisions, we needed to know what the future would be like. As I look back at what actually happened, our expectations were pretty good, as good as anyone could expect without a crystal ball.

We didn't foresee how much technology or international commerce would change. Back then, the company was rated as the "Best Managed Company in the United States." But now, unable to adjust to all the changes, the company is having serious financial problems. Apparently, managers quit looking at the future strategically. Their values changed. Gold became more important than the Golden Rule.

Changes Ahead

The rate of change in our world is now moving at such a rapid pace, anticipating life twenty years from now would have to look like something out of a science fiction novel—possibly real, but probably not. But something even greater and more unbelievable may exist. What we once might have projected as happening in twenty years could easily come in the next five.

E-books, audio books, and online magazines and newspapers may replace most print media. Voice recognition software will allow hands-free electronic communication to just about anyone worldwide, with a computer immediately answering questions and responding to commands.

Where we work, how we work, and why we work will adjust to changing times. Computers can recognize faces, conduct research, and diagnose cancer faster and more reliably than humans.

Each year, people's average lifespan increases. It doesn't seem that long ago when most people didn't live much past age seventy. In another twenty years at the present rate, we might see lots of centenarians jogging around the neighborhood parks.

World Demographics

Oceans and undeveloped land were once vast enough to separate nations. People were content to live in the communities where they were born.

The global media via the Internet and cell phones has now made it possible for most people to see outside their world. They are often led to believe the grass might be greener in a foreign country on the other side of the fence.

Immigration, not births, is flooding our country with population growth, and minorities may soon become the majority. With these changes, our world cannot possibly remain the same.

Threat from Foreign Countries

More countries are acquiring nuclear abilities that make them an unpredictable threat to world peace. Terrorism is now a global concern, and suspense-filled movies remind us that one crazy person might destroy a nation.

The Internet has provided a platform for stirring anger and strife that can lead to violence and war. With all the firewalls and data security created by our software developers, foreign governments still find a way to steal technology, access top secrets, and influence

222

public opinion. If they can, they will add confusion to political campaigns and possibly change the outcome of our elections.

Friendly Competition

As a puppy, a wolf might appear to be man's best friend, but when it's fully grown and independent, it might bite your hand off. I'm afraid some countries that seem to be so friendly could one day call for our destruction.

Thirty years ago, I started doing business in China. With their hand labor so unbelievably cheap, we could trade our dollars for goods that would be three or four times more expensive if produced in America. Over the years, they acquired our technology and methods and made them better, to the point that our own economy is threatened. The rise of Chinese technology, economics, and military strength built on capitalism principles have made the country a less-than-friendly competitor.

American Political Values

Every year that this country moves away from capitalism values and embraces more socialism, we avoid the challenges that must be faced.

I believe it was Abraham Lincoln who expressed concerns about our country's future with observations like these:

- The poor cannot be helped by destroying the rich.
- The weak are not strengthened by weakening the strong.
- Prosperity cannot be built by discouraging thrift.
- The wage earner cannot be lifted up by pulling the wage payer down.
- The brotherhood of man cannot be advanced by inciting class hatred.
- Character and courage cannot be developed by taking away people's initiative and independence.
- People aren't permanently better off when we do for them what they could do for themselves."

The longer we wait on the solutions, the bigger the problems will be.

The Debate

I heard a debate on the biggest threats for our grandchildren. I was surprised. And not surprised.

One debater blamed the culture and values that want to get more but don't want to give, which is fundamentally opposed to old-fashioned capitalism and free enterprise.

The other debater pointed to our educational system that is moving away from the old-fashioned self-reliance and achievement values to a world of inclusion, without competition, where everybody gets a trophy. We complain about not having enough and preach a religion of self-gratification. He said our colleges and universities have moved far away from old-fashioned values.

Which is it, the culture influencing the education system or education influencing the culture? Either way, as long as it sounds good to the young mind, the socialism message will keep spreading until some very strong arguments stand against it.

In 1959, I heard Nikita Khrushchev of the Soviet Union say, "Your children's children will live under communism." He wasn't declaring war. He was predicting our economic and social collapse that would lead our youth to embrace communism. If he were alive today, he might see enough socialism to say, "See, I told you so."

Turning Point

We cannot walk together and go in different directions (Amos 3:3). Socialism takes us on a much different path from capitalism and free enterprise. The direction we choose will determine the future for our grandchildren and generations to come.

We can have great leadership when we turn our attention to some of the old-fashioned values that spurred the growth of our country for two centuries. But we must have the courage to take the actions necessary to reverse the alarming trends toward greed and standards that oppose biblical principles.

Like peace-loving lambs who roar like lions, our God-centered faith needs to be amplified. We should have some serious conversations with God about who he wants us to be and what we should be doing to fulfill his purpose. We should pray as Jesus once prayed: "Your kingdom come, your will be done, on Earth as it is in Heaven" (Matthew 6:10).

Stand-Up Values

Be sure to fear the Lord and serve him faithfully
with all your heart; consider what great things
he has done for you. — 1 Samuel 12:24

I do not pretend to be an expert on values, but I am quite familiar with what Jesus said, which pointed the way to the "way, truth, and life." My success in managing businesses has come from respecting the Ten Commandments and the biblical principles of love and service.

Help along the Way

Truth is something to be discovered, not debated. Jesus said God's Spirit was sent to guide us to the truth (John 16:13). We will not figure it out on our own. We need his help.

God has been in this old-fashioned value business for a very long time. The Bible presents foundational values that make businesses and relationships thrive, but they need to move from the printed page to our hearts and minds. If that happens, we can change the world, and right now, our world is in desperate need of change.

The Great Challenge

Among the last words spoken while on Earth, Jesus said, "Go into all the world and preach the gospel to all creation" (Mark 16:15). We should not restrict the meaning of that exhortation to ministers of the Church. We should always be ready to express the hope that lies within us (1 Peter 3:15), hidden until we speak up.

Studies have suggested that people's number-one fear is speaking. Whenever we imagine the slightest chance of conflict, we think silence is golden. But actually, silence is fool's gold. If we are wise and want to live, we *must* open up and share our convictions.

Our moral and social systems are being challenged as never before. If we remain a part of the "silent majority," we proclaim a non-existent message, because it cannot be heard. It's time to grab the bullhorn away from the 3 percent and spread our good news where it cannot be missed.

My Prayer

The prayers of righteous people make a difference (James 5:16), and I have great hope for you. I pray that you will . . .

- Have the desire, knowledge, and wisdom to promote the values to make our country a better place.
- Enjoy the same kind of rich and full lives that my wife and I have had in our wonderful country.
- Take part in building a great future for yourselves and our country.
- Use the gifts God has given to you to fulfill his purpose for your life.
- Find true love in your lives, which is even greater than faith and hope (1 Corinthians 13:13).
- Turn all your stumbling blocks into stepping stones.

The road to success isn't easy, but it's worth all the hard effort.

Yes, You Can

In any and every situation, whether well fed or hungry,
whether living in plenty or in want, I can do all this
through him who gives me strength. — Philippians 4:12–13

Sometimes people look at me as if they wish they could have the wonderful experiences I've had. Is that possible? I don't think so, because they aren't me. If people only knew, they should be excited about that, not disappointed.

Land of Opportunity

If I could start at the beginning and live my life over again, it would be entirely different now, because circumstances are nothing like they used to be. Some things would be easier, but I would also face problems that could never have been solved before. But solutions are possible now.

You won't have the same opportunities that I had, but that's good news, not bad. Different opportunities will arise for you, which you may handle with ease—if you're ready. That's where you could use some help from my old-fashioned values.

We used to have an old saying: "Opportunity doesn't knock twice." That meant we needed to be ready, always studying, learning, preparing for the day when we could open the door and welcome unexpected success.

Modern values lead us to wait for an opportunity. When it comes, then we'll prepare, but that's too late.

Preparing for the Unknown

All my great successes were preceded by failures that taught me some very important lessons on how to succeed. I've tried and failed many times. In the old days, failure was just an expected part of progress, but more people today seem to fear failure so much that they won't even try. You'll never be a success unless you can allow yourself to fail.

Without a doubt, the most important reason for my success was asking for God's guidance all along the way. Surviving the Great Depression was worse than being homeless, because there was no place to beg. It seemed that everybody was out of work and hungry. Nobody had any money. With so many of our boys being killed for our freedom, two world wars brought greater challenges than what the history books describe. Without God's comfort and pointing to the next step I needed to take, life would not have been so good.

The Right Dependency

Today, too many capable people are dependent on the government for benefits. If they would do all they can, they would learn and become stronger, able to do more and prosper. But their dependency keeps them weak.

If we can see ourselves as God's creation, put on Earth for a purpose, we can be sure he will walk with us as we do the good we know to do. I believe this is what spurred this country's development over the first two hundred years, making it the greatest in the world. Our dependency on God, not government, has been the foundation for our success.

The Value of Work

Whoever said life should be easy didn't know what he was talking about. Success comes at a high price: we call it *work*. Actually, it requires *hard* work. No, it's *very* hard work. I hope you get the point. We scrimp and save, making sacrifices, and strain with all our might, and for what? The reward we believe lies ahead.

If we don't believe in the value of work, we'll never do it. We'll be satisfied to live on government welfare and wonder why everybody else is having all the fun.

We must believe in the reward, or we won't make the sacrifices that prepare us for the opportunities ahead. After Jesus' disciples witnessed countless miracles—the deaf hearing, the blind seeing, the wind and waves calmed, the dead raised to life—they heard Jesus say, "You'll do greater works than these" (John 14:12).

To be successful, you must do the work, and to do the work, you must believe in the value.

No Retreat

I believe you will see many opportunities that I never saw in my lifetime. We don't have to look very far to see how great the needs and problems are. Study hard and work hard, and you will help solve them.

Jesus said that those who put their hand to the plow and look back are not worthy of the Kingdom of God (Luke 9:62). The past with all its successes built on old-fashioned values are only of use in moving forward, not going back. Legend says that when Captain Cortés landed in Veracruz in 1519, he ordered the ships burned so his men would know they could only press forward. There was no going back.

Failure is never final unless we choose to give up. Quitting should never be an option. If you keep getting up, you will learn from your mistakes and become stronger. You probably won't see the success of all your dreams, but you're sure to experience the smaller successes that become stepping stones to something greater.

Possibility Thinking

Dr. Robert Schuller became well known for his "possibility thinking." We don't know what the future holds, but there's a natural tendency to work toward what we believe. If we see ourselves failing, odds are good that we will.

I don't endorse the idea that we can have whatever we dream. That's not always realistic. But because I believe in God's miraculous power, I can trust what Jesus said: "With God, all things are possible" (Matthew 19:26).

For forty years, I have carried Dr. Schuller's "Possibility Thinkers Creed" on a scrap of paper in my wallet, as a reminder: *When faced with a mountain, I will not quit. I will keep on striving until I climb over, find a pass through, tunnel underneath—or simply stay and turn the mountain into a gold mine, with God's help.*

Can you face all of the challenges? Can you establish the values needed for great times? Can you make the world a better place? Will you enjoy success? With God's help, yes. You can.

Jack Bush

Jack Bush has had a pretty good life. From humble beginnings, he has come a long way—with God's help.

He has been president, CEO, or board member of many large companies. As president of Michaels, he was influential in seeing the small struggling company deep in debt grow to the country's largest retailer of arts and crafts products. He was founder and chairman of several start-up companies including IdeaForest.com and Artistree. In his retirement years, he has been active as a consultant or CEO for several "problem companies" during periods of reorganization.

Jack and his wife, Mary, generously support ministries in their church and their community. Jack is still active with the University of Missouri and has served on various boards and chaired several. He and Mary have been honored for their support with the Jack and Mary Bush Auditorium and the beautiful four-story atrium in the College of Business,

He believes strongly that his family, and especially his grandchildren, should understand their heritage and have books to pass on to future generations. He has published six books of family lives, times, and history, including *Sarah Bush Lincoln*.

Jack and Mary are committed Christians—members of the King of Glory Lutheran Church and the Roaring Lambs Bible Study. They believe the greatest values of life come from God and feel those values should be amplified.

Frank Ball

For ten years, Frank Ball directed North Texas Christian Writers to help members improve their writing and storytelling skills. In 2011, he founded Story Help Groups and joined the Roaring Writers ministry seven years later to encourage and equip all Christians to tell their life-changing stories. He has taught at writer's conferences and churches across the U.S. and Canada. Besides writing his own books, he does ghostwriting, copy editing, and graphic design to help others publish high-quality books.

As Pastor of Biblical Research and Writing for three years, he wrote sermons, teaching materials, and hundreds of devotions. He coaches writers, writes blogs, and is a panelist on The Writer's View. His first book, *Eyewitness: The Life of Christ Told in One Story*, is a compilation of biblical information on the life of Christ in a chronological story that reads like a novel. His website is www.FrankBall.org.

60773033R00137

Made in the USA
Middletown, DE
16 August 2019